RISE TO YOUR FULL POTENTIAL

Jagdip Punia

INDIA · SINGAPORE · MALAYSIA

ISBN 979-8-89446-069-7

Contents

With gratitude for their unwavering commitment, this book is dedicated to the brave men and women of the police force.

"To the steadfast guardians of our communities, Whose courage and dedication illuminate even the darkest of days.

May your tireless service continue to inspire and protect."

Chapter 1

Why Rise to Your Full Potential

Sheetal Devi's story is a powerful example of turning challenges into opportunities. As a para-archer, she embodies resilience and determination, showing us that obstacles can be overcome with perseverance and passion. Her journey goes beyond sports, offering a lesson in facing adversity head-on.

Starting with the basics—a bow and arrows—and facing physical challenges, Sheetal didn't let her circumstances hold her back. She practiced with what she had, showing us that it's your willpower, not your resources, that defines your success. Her achievements are remarkable, having won 2 golds and 1 silver medal in the Asian Para Games 2022, and she was awarded the prestigious Arjuna Award at the tender age of just 16 years.

Her life encourages us to pursue our dreams relentlessly. It proves that with persistence, you can go beyond your limitations and achieve greatness.

As we get to know more about Sheetal Devi, we see a clear message: success is about moving forward, step by step, toward your goals, no matter how unreachable they might seem at first.

"Discipline is the bridge between goals and accomplishment".
- Jim Rohn

Life's clarity and stability

In the journey of life, clarity and stability often seem like distant goals. Picture, for a moment, a simple tripod standing steady on three legs. Each leg represents a crucial part of our lives: our health and happiness, our connections with people, and the work or passions we pursue. Just like a tripod needs all three legs to stand, we need these three aspects of our lives to be in harmony to feel stable and secure.

Now, think about the banyan tree, with its vast network of branches and roots. It's more than just a tree; it's a living, growing symbol of strength. The most fascinating thing about the banyan tree is its aerial roots, which grow down from the branches into the ground, forming new support systems. Over time, this single tree can spread out, creating a whole forest of its own.

This idea of the banyan tree mirrors our own personal growth. Stability doesn't mean standing still. Just like the banyan tree spreads its roots to grow wider and stronger, we too can reach out in new directions, learn new skills, face challenges, and make new connections. Each new experience or skill is like an aerial root, helping us become more resilient and adaptable.

Combining these two images, the tripod and the banyan tree, offers a fresh way to look at our lives. The tripod reminds us to keep our lives balanced, making sure we don't ignore our health, our relationships, or our work. The banyan tree inspires us to keep growing, to reach out and establish new roots. It teaches us that being stable doesn't mean staying in one place; it means being strong enough to grow and adapt.

As we move through life, let's aim to be like both the tripod and the banyan tree. Let's work on keeping our lives balanced while also being open to growth and change. By doing this, we can achieve the clarity and stability we are searching for, building a life that's both grounded and constantly evolving.

Why learn new skills

Learning new skills is the solid foundation of personal and professional stability. Think of this process as evolving through different modes of transportation, from a unicycle to a car. Each stage represents a leap in capability, offering a clear lens through which we can view the importance of skill acquisition, especially for individuals across diverse business industries.

Starting with the unicycle, the initial challenge is balance. In business, this mirrors the early stages of learning a new skill—navigating uncertainty with focus and determination. The unicycle phase is tough; it's where the groundwork is laid, and the foundation for all future skills is built. Here, the lesson is about perseverance, an essential quality for any individual aiming to go through uncharted waters.

Progressing to a bicycle with two wheels, suddenly, there's a bit more stability. You're trying to stay upright; you're learning to steer, to navigate. In your career, this is near to building upon that initial skill, adding another layer of expertise. You're more stable now, moving with a bit more confidence, exploring further afield as your capabilities grow.

Advancing to a motorbike, stability is no longer the main concern. Now, it's about mastering control, about efficiency and speed. In the professional space, this translates to honing your skills to the point where you're competent; you're proficient. You understand the nuances of your tasks, you're more productive, and you can handle more complex challenges with ease.

Finally, driving a car represents the culmination of skill acquisition. The journey from the unicycle to the car is a journey of increasing complexity, speed, and stability. Each step along the way adds a branch of skill, confidence, and capability. In the workplace, mastering a new skill set is similar to adding another wheel to your vehicle. With each new skill, you're moving faster; you're navigating the professional landscape with greater assurance and the ability to take on more complex tasks. You become more agile and valuable to your organisation, to your community, to your family and team.

In an ever-evolving marketplace, the ability to adapt, to learn, and to grow is what sets apart the successful from the stagnant. For employees, acquiring new skills means job security and potential for career advancement. For businesses, it's the difference between staying relevant and falling behind.

In the journey of lifelong learning, each new skill acquired is a step towards greater stability and speed in navigating the complexities of the professional world. Just like moving from a unicycle to a car, the path to mastery is built on the willingness to embrace the initial instability, to learn, to grow, and to eventually drive forward with confidence and control. This is not about personal achievement; it's about contributing to a team, a company, and an industry's forward momentum.

Importance of skill acquisition

Learning new skills is not about adding bullet points to a resume; it's about laying down bricks to build a more robust foundation for both professional and personal life. Think of each new skill as a brick. On its own, it might not seem like much, but together, these bricks form the sturdy base upon which careers and lives are built and expanded.

The purpose of acquiring new skills goes beyond immediate utility. It's about creating a reservoir of knowledge and capability that can be drawn upon in times of need. For instance, learning to communicate effectively is not about being able to present ideas clearly; it's also about being able to negotiate better, resolve conflicts, and build stronger relationships. Similarly, developing project management skills can help organise one's personal goals and commitments with the same efficiency applied to professional projects.

Adding value through skills is a pathway to personal achievement but a means to contribute more significantly to teams, organisations, and communities. It's about enhancing one's ability to solve problems, to innovate, and to adapt to new challenges. This opens new opportunities for advancement and also enriches personal life, offering new perspectives, hobbies, and ways to engage with the world.

In essence, skill acquisition is about building a foundation that offers stability and flexibility to navigate the winds of change. It's about not only oneself for the next step in a career, but also the unexpected twists and turns of a lifetime. This approach to learning and growth ensures that, no matter what challenges lie ahead, the foundation you've built will support you, enabling you to reach new heights and explore new horizons.

The Eiffel Tower Analogy

When we think about building something that lasts, something that reaches high into the sky like the Eiffel Tower, we're reminded of the importance of a strong foundation. Just as the Eiffel Tower stands tall and proud against the Paris skyline, its strength and stability come from the solid base it's built upon. This principle applies directly to our journey of learning and skill acquisition.

Imagine trying to construct a skyscraper on a shaky foundation. No matter how impressive the design or the materials, it won't stand the test of time or weather the storms. The same goes for our professional and personal development. Without a solid base of skills, we might reach a certain height, but we'll be vulnerable to the slightest change in the wind.

The process of building this foundation starts with the essentials, the core skills that every role requires. Just as architects and engineers pour concrete and lay steel to create a stable base for the Eiffel Tower, we too, must invest time and effort into developing these foundational skills. These could range from technical know-how specific to our field to softer skills like communication, teamwork, and critical thinking.

The beauty of the Eiffel Tower is not in its height or its iconic structure; it's also in its ability to last. Over the years, it has withstood storms, cold, and heat, remaining a constant symbol of Paris. In our careers and lives, we aim for a similar kind of resilience. By regularly learning and strengthening our skill set, we ensure that we can reach great heights and also sustain ourselves there, regardless of what challenges come our way.

Reaching our fullest potential is much like erecting the Eiffel Tower: it begins with thoughtful planning and a commitment to laying a strong foundation, enriched by constantly adding new skills for stability and growth. A well-built skill set paves the way for immediate achievements, which forges a legacy that endures, echoing the timeless stature of the Eiffel Tower.

Chapter 2

Choose Your Skills

Identifying Skills to Acquire

Let's start with a simple scene: you, a notepad, and a pen. This isn't just another day of listing tasks. Today, you're charting out the future, skill by skill. This might not be done in one session but may take up to three sessions without distractions. But here's the twist – it's a brainstorming session unlike any other. Think of it as throwing everything on the wall to see what sticks, but with a bit more strategy behind it.

First off, let's acknowledge something important. Your mood, the news you read this morning, the last conversation you had – it all plays into this. It's like picking a movie to watch; what you choose on a lazy Sunday might be worlds apart from a midweek pick-me-up. This session is all about embracing that fluidity, and understanding that today's passion project could be tomorrow's old news. And that's okay.

Now, imagine listing every skill that's ever made your ears perk up, from speaking a new language to coding, from baking to blockchain. Let them flow without judgement. It's a bit like scrolling through your favourite streaming service, adding anything that catches your eye to your watchlist. Except here, you're curating skills, not shows.

But here's the catch – not every skill makes the cut for the next round. This is where the funnel narrows, and you start to sift through your list. Think about what aligns with your life right now, what fits into your schedule, and what gets you excited to learn. It's a bit like deciding whether to invest your time in starting a new series or rewatching an old favourite. You're looking for that perfect match that feels both exciting and doable.

The goal here isn't to walk away with a mile-long list but to pinpoint a handful of skills that really speak to you. It's about quality over quantity, choosing paths that light up a spark inside you. And it's not just about the skill itself but about what it represents – a step towards a new version of you that's just on the horizon, waiting to be discovered.

So, as you wrap up the final session, you're not just leaving with a list. You're stepping out with a clearer vision of where you want to go and how you plan to get there. It's about setting the stage for growth, exploration, and the kind of personal development that doesn't just happen overnight. It's a commitment to yourself, to keep pushing, keep learning, and keep evolving, no matter what life throws your way.

And remember, this is just the beginning. The real adventure starts with what you do next.

The fluidity of priorities and interests

Understanding how our priorities and interests evolve over time is crucial, especially when it comes to learning and personal development. It's a natural progression, like seasons changing throughout the year, each bringing its own set of activities and moods.

However, as time passes, the focus often shifts. You might find yourself drawn to professional skills, intrigued by the challenge of mastering a new software or improving your communication abilities. This transition from personal to professional development isn't a sign of fickleness but an indication of growth. Life is dynamic, filled with endless opportunities for learning and advancement. Our interests naturally evolve in response to this dynamism, influenced by our experiences, interactions, and the changing world around us.

Embracing this fluidity is essential. Imagine walking through a forest; the path twists and turns, offering various directions to explore. Similarly, our journey of skill acquisition is not linear. It meanders, allowing us to explore different facets of our personalities and capabilities. This exploration is enriching, leading to a well-rounded and versatile skill set.

Self-reflection plays a pivotal role in navigating this journey. Regularly taking stock of our goals, interests, and what we genuinely need at any given moment helps keep us aligned with our aspirations. It's not about rigidly sticking to a predefined path but about being open to new directions that resonate with our evolving selves.

In essence, the development of our interests and priorities is a continuous, dynamic process. It mirrors life's complexity, filled with shifts and turns that reflect our growing understanding of ourselves and the world. By staying adaptable and open to change, we can navigate this journey effectively, ensuring that our learning and growth are both meaningful and fulfilling.

Prioritising Skills

Prioritising skills for organic upskilling requires a strategic approach, focusing on enhancing and complementing existing strengths for cohesive professional growth. This process is directly linked to understanding the specific demands and future directions of various industries, ensuring that employees across diverse business fronts can remain competitive and innovative.

For instance, an IT professional specialising in software development might prioritise learning cloud computing technologies. This decision is informed by the growing shift towards cloud-based solutions across industries, from finance to healthcare. By acquiring skills in cloud infrastructure and services, the professional not only deepens their expertise in a complementary area but also aligns their skill set with emerging industry standards and demands.

Similarly, a project manager working in construction could benefit from upskilling in sustainable building practices. With a global push towards sustainability, understanding green construction techniques and energy-efficient design becomes a strategic asset. This new skill set not only enhances the manager's ability to lead projects that meet modern sustainability standards but also positions them as a forward-thinking leader in their field.

In the creative industries, a graphic designer might choose to upskill in user experience (UX) design. This decision reflects an understanding of the digital landscape's evolution, where engaging user interfaces are crucial for success. By integrating UX design principles into their skill set, the designer can create more impactful, user-centered designs, bridging visual aesthetics with functional usability.

The process of selecting which skills to prioritise also involves a thorough analysis of personal career goals and industry trends. This may include reviewing employment market data, consulting with mentors, and participating in professional networks to gauge which skills are most valuable and in demand.

Developing "T" skills is crucial. The vertical line symbolises deep expertise, discipline, and knowledge in a specific field, while the horizontal line signifies versatile competencies and the capacity to collaborate across various roles.

Moreover, the commitment to upskilling should be matched with a practical plan for learning. This might involve setting aside dedicated time for online courses, workshops, or hands-on projects. The goal is to achieve a balance between current job responsibilities and learning new skills, ensuring steady progress without overwhelming oneself.

Ultimately, the act of prioritising skills for upskilling is a dynamic and ongoing process. It requires professionals to be proactive, reflective, and adaptable, continually assessing their skills against the backdrop of industry developments and personal career aspirations. By focusing on skills that complement and enhance their existing strengths, individuals can achieve more cohesive and impactful growth, positioning themselves as valuable contributors in their fields.

"Transformation with convenience is not possible. Conviction and convenience can not stay under one roof. You have to sign off for inconvenience."

– Lisa Nichols

Narrowing Down Choices

Narrowing down choices to one by one skills that align with current abilities and professional needs is a critical step in the upskilling process. This stage demands a focused evaluation of one's career trajectory, the market's direction, and the realistic assessment of one's capacity to learn and integrate new skills effectively.

The first step in this filtering process involves a thorough self-assessment. Professionals need to take stock of their current skill set, identifying areas of strength and potential gaps. This introspection helps in understanding which new skills would seamlessly integrate with existing competencies, thereby enhancing overall professional value. For example, a web developer proficient in front-end technologies might consider learning back-end development to become a full-stack developer, thus significantly increasing their marketability and project handling capability.

Next, it's crucial to align skill selection with professional needs. This involves looking at industry trends, skill enhancement is not to change jobs, but to be of more value to the stakeholders. For instance, a marketing professional might notice a surge in demand for digital marketing skills such as SEO or analytics. Choosing to upskill in these areas not only aligns with the current market demand but also positions the individual for future advancements.

The selection process also requires prioritising skills based on their potential impact on career growth. This means evaluating each skill not just for its immediate benefits but also for its long-term value. Skills that offer the possibility of opening new career paths or leadership opportunities should be given precedence. For example, learning project management methodologies can be a game-changer for someone looking to move into leadership roles.

Additionally, practical considerations play a significant role in narrowing down choices. Time, resources, and the learning curve associated with acquiring new skills must be realistically assessed. It's essential to choose skills that can be realistically developed within one's current lifestyle and work commitments. Setting ambitious but achievable goals ensures that the upskilling process is motivating rather than overwhelming.

Finally, after considering all these factors, it's time to make the tough choices. This decision-making process involves ranking the selected skills based on their relevance, impact, and feasibility. The goal is to arrive at a focused list of one skill at a time that promises the most significant benefit to one's career development.

In conclusion, narrowing down skill choices is a deliberate process that balances personal interests with professional requirements and market trends. By selecting skills that build on existing strengths and align with future opportunities, professionals can ensure that their upskilling efforts are both effective and rewarding.

Focus is the key

The importance of focus in the upskilling journey cannot be overstated. It's the difference between spreading one's efforts too thinly across many areas, like a gun spraying multiple lasers in different directions, and channeling all energy into a single, impactful direction, akin to a laser focused on a precise target. This focused approach ensures that the effort invested in learning and development yields the highest possible returns.

When professionals scatter their attention across too many skills simultaneously, they risk diluting their efforts. Each skill, like each laser beam from a gun, requires a certain amount of energy and time to develop. Spreading resources too thin means that none of the skills gets enough attention to develop to a level where it can significantly impact one's career. It's akin to lighting several small fires hoping one might catch, but in reality, all you get is smoke.

On the other hand, applying a single laser focus to learning allows for deep, meaningful engagement with the material. This focused approach facilitates not just the acquisition of a new skill but also its integration into one's existing skill set, enhancing overall performance and expertise. It's about choosing to start a controlled burn that has the power to clear a path forward, rather than dissipating one's efforts in multiple directions.

The effectiveness of a single laser focus is evident in the mastery it allows one to achieve. Mastery is not just about understanding a skill on the surface but about gaining a deep, intuitive grasp of its nuances, applications, and potential for innovation. This level of understanding can only be achieved through focused effort and dedication.

Moreover, focusing on one skill at a time allows for the application of learning in real-world scenarios, which is crucial for cementing new knowledge. It provides the opportunity to experiment, make mistakes, and learn from them, thereby deepening one's understanding and ability to apply the skill creatively and effectively in various contexts.

The focused approach also aligns with the principle of quality over quantity. In a professional landscape that values expertise and specialisation, a range of skills are required. This specialisation enables professionals to carve out unique niches for themselves, making them indispensable in their fields.

In essence, the importance of focus in upskilling is about making strategic choices that align with one's career goals, dedicating the necessary time and resources to achieve mastery, and applying learned skills in a way that significantly impacts one's professional trajectory. By comparing the effectiveness of a single laser focus to a gun with multiple lasers, it's clear that a concentrated effort not only enhances skill acquisition but also propels career growth in a more meaningful and impactful direction.

Commitment and Regular Practice

The initial rush of excitement when starting to learn something new is natural, but it's the steady, ongoing dedication that turns a budding interest into a deeply ingrained skill. Commitment and regular practice are the bedrock of truly mastering new skills.

The challenge many face is maintaining motivation beyond the initial enthusiasm. As the novelty wears off and the hard work sets in, it's tempting to move on to the next exciting thing. However, the key to real growth and development lies in sticking with it, even when the going gets tough.

Consider the process of learning to play a musical instrument. The early stages, where every note is a discovery, can feel exhilarating. But as progress requires more nuanced and repetitive practice, the initial thrill may diminish. It's at this stage that commitment becomes crucial. Setting aside regular practice time, focusing on small improvements, and gradually increasing the complexity of pieces played transforms sporadic effort into skillfulness.

This principle applies across all skill learning. Whether it's coding, a new language, or a professional competency like public speaking, the pattern is the same. After the excitement fades, what remains is the routine of practice. This routine, far from being mundane, is where the magic happens. It's in the repeated application and practice of a skill that deep learning and integration into one's repertoire occur.

Creating a structured schedule can help in maintaining this commitment. Allocating specific times for practice and sticking to them builds a habit. Over time, this habit becomes second nature, and the skill being practised becomes a part of who you are.

Moreover, setting realistic goals can keep motivation high. Instead of aiming for broad, undefined mastery, setting clear, achievable milestones can provide a sense of progress and accomplishment. Celebrating these small victories can renew enthusiasm, making regular practice less of a chore and more of a journey with visible progress.

It's also helpful to remind oneself of the long-term benefits of sticking with a skill. Beyond the immediate gains in knowledge and ability, developing a deep, comprehensive skill set can open new professional doors, enhance personal satisfaction, and even boost self-confidence.

The Benefits of High Commitment

Virat Kohli. Kohli's career provides a tangible insight into how fluctuations in dedication can impact performance and self-belief, and how recommitting oneself can lead to a remarkable turnaround.

Virat Kohli, who made his international debut for the Indian cricket team in 2008, quickly rose to prominence due to his exceptional talent and aggressive playing style. However, despite his early success, Kohli faced a period where his performance suffered. This phase, around 2014, was marked by a significant drop in his batting averages, especially during the England tour, where he struggled to score runs. The root cause wasn't just technical flaws; it was also a decreased commitment to rigorous practice and physical fitness, which had been pillars of his initial success.

In response, Kohli embarked on a transformative journey that involved a renewed commitment to practice, a strict fitness regime, and a focus on mental health. He recognized that talent alone wasn't enough; it needed to be supported by relentless dedication and discipline. By adopting a rigorous training schedule, focusing on his diet, and addressing the mental aspects of his game, Kohli managed to turn his career around dramatically.

This renewed commitment translated into remarkable performances on the field. Kohli's comeback was not just a return to form but a path to new heights, breaking numerous records and earning accolades worldwide. His journey from a dip in form to becoming one of the best batsmen in the world is a testament to the power of dedication and the positive impact it can have on confidence.

Chapter 3

Plan for Resources

Understanding Learning Formats

Choosing how we learn is a lot like picking a route on a long journey. You've got three main roads: formal learning, informal learning, and a mix of both, which we call hybrid learning.

Formal learning is the classic classroom setup. It's all about signing up for a course, going through lessons, and getting that certificate at the end. It's straightforward, like following a recipe to the letter. You know exactly what ingredients you need, how long it's going to take, and what the outcome should be. It's great for those who like a clear plan and seeing a tangible reward for their efforts.

Then there's informal learning. This one doesn't come with sign-up sheets or diplomas. It happens as you go about your day, tackling real-world problems at work or picking up new skills on the fly. It's like learning to cook by experimenting with ingredients you have on hand. Sometimes you might end up with something amazing, and other times, it's just about gaining the experience. This approach suits the curious minds who love to explore and aren't afraid of a few surprises along the way.

Hybrid learning is where things get interesting. It combines the structured aspect of formal courses with the flexibility of informal learning. Imagine you're learning to cook by following a recipe but also throwing in a few twists of your own. You have a solid foundation but with enough room to play and make it your own. This method is perfect for those who appreciate a bit of guidance but also want the freedom to apply what they learn in their own unique way.

So, when it comes down to deciding how you want to learn, think about what suits you best. Do you prefer a clear path laid out in front of you, the thrill of discovering things on your own, or a bit of both? There's no right or wrong answer here; it's all about what matches your style and how you can best absorb new information and skills.

Organic Learning

Organic learning is about integrating structured education with your personal or professional life in a way that feels natural and directly applicable. This method involves engaging with formal education—like certification courses—that aligns closely with your current job or future career aspirations. For instance, if you are in a technical field, taking a course in advanced software engineering that offers both a deep understanding and a practical certification can significantly enhance your skills in a meaningful way.

This approach is beneficial because it combines the rigor of formal education with the practicality of everyday work. It's not about collecting credentials but about making tangible improvements to your abilities and understanding. This form of learning ensures you are not just passively absorbing information but actively applying it in your daily professional life, making it a deeply integrated and organic process.

Inorganic Learning

Inorganic learning is about exploring knowledge and skills outside your everyday work or personal interests. It involves engaging with diverse sources like books, podcasts, YouTube videos, seminars, exhibitions, and even social media posts. This type of learning is less about direct application in your day-to-day tasks and more about broadening your perspective and understanding different contexts and fields.

This form of learning is crucial because it builds a versatile knowledge base, helping you become more adaptable and innovative. Engaging with various media and platforms exposes you to new ideas and trends that can indirectly influence your primary field of work or spark new interests.

It requires a mindset open to learning for the sake of learning, appreciating the intrinsic value of knowledge. While the skills and information might not directly impact your current job, they equip you with a broader understanding that can be crucial in unexpected ways, fostering long-term intellectual growth and curiosity.

For Example, Organic Learning

Organic learning involves acquiring skills that are directly related to one's current job role, often through formal certifications. This type of learning is integrated into daily work activities, providing immediate and practical benefits.

★ **Stores Person:** Undertaking formal certifications in "Warehouse Management" or "Inventory Management." These certifications allow the individual to apply learned skills directly in their daily job, enhancing their ability to manage inventory effectively.

- ★ **Quality Assurance Personnel:** Earning a certification in "Quality Management Systems" to directly improve their oversight of product quality.
- ★ **Production Worker:** Gaining formal qualifications in "Production Planning and Control" to optimize production efficiency.
- ★ **Purchasing Officer:** Completing courses in "Supply Chain Management" to better manage supplier relations and procurement processes.

Inorganic Learning

Inorganic learning refers to acquiring skills or knowledge through educational means that are not directly related to one's daily job functions. This type of learning involves gaining qualifications or knowledge in areas outside of one's usual professional scope, which might not have immediate practical applications in their current role but can broaden one's skill set.

- ★ **Maintenance Worker Learning Digital Marketing:** While this skill does not directly enhance their ability to maintain machinery or manage facilities, it could be useful for personal projects or career changes.
- ★ **Engineer Studying Fine Arts:** Learning about fine arts may not impact an engineer's day-to-day tasks but can enhance creative thinking and provide a mental break from their technical routine.
- ★ **HR Professional Learning Coding:** Through formal courses, an HR professional may learn coding, which isn't essential for typical HR tasks but could be beneficial for automated system management or transitioning into tech-based roles in HR systems.

The Pitfalls of High-Sounding Courses

When people eye certifications like Six Sigma Black Belt, there's a bit of dazzle to it. Imagine walking through a factory and seeing those "Zero PPM" posters everywhere. It's almost like a badge of honour, a promise of perfection in manufacturing. But, let's take a step back and think about it. Who really benefits more here? I'd wager that the folks printing those posters might just be the biggest winners, financially speaking.

Now, don't get me wrong. I'm not saying Six Sigma or other similar courses don't have their merits. They teach valuable skills in process improvement and quality control that can make a big difference. But here's the kicker: it's all about how relevant these skills are to what you're actually doing on the factory floor.

You see, having a bunch of Six Sigma Black Belts in a plant doesn't automatically mean you're going to hit that Zero PPM target. It's not that straightforward. The real question is, how do these skills apply to the daily grind? How do they help solve the real problems you face?

The appeal of these courses often comes down to the prestige they carry, the idea of joining an elite club committed to making things better. And that's great, as long as it's not just about the prestige. The true value comes from putting those skills to work, from making a real difference in how things run.

So, when thinking about diving into something like Six Sigma, it pays to be a bit critical. Ask yourself how it will help in the specific context of your work. It's not just about adding another line to your resume or another certificate to the wall. It's about making sure those efforts lead to real improvements, to tackling those challenges head-on.

While I don't oppose Six Sigma courses, their relevance is crucial.

Delving further into certifications, it's important to move our attention from the appeal of the certificate to what it actually signifies.: relevance and practical application. In the bustling ecosystem of professional development, where certifications are often seen as golden tickets to career advancement, the real gold lies not in the certificate but in the actionable skills it signifies.

Imagine you're at the crossroads of deciding which course to take. On one side, there's a path leading to a certification that's buzzing with popularity, its name echoing through the corridors of your workplace. On the other, a less trodden path focusing on skills directly applicable to your daily challenges. The choice might seem daunting, but when you strip away the prestige and focus on what will truly elevate your capabilities, the decision becomes clearer.

The heart of the matter is practicality. Think about the tools and techniques that will directly impact your work. It's about learning something today that you can apply tomorrow. This hands-on knowledge not only boosts your confidence but also elevates your value within your team and organisation.

Certifications should be more than just a decorative badge of honour; they should be a testament to your ability to tackle real-world problems with competence and finesse. It's the difference between knowing the theory behind driving a car and actually being able to navigate the bustling streets of a busy city.

In the grand scheme of things, the spotlight shouldn't just shine on the certificate but on the journey it represents—a journey of growth, learning, and most importantly, application. As you weigh your options, remember, the most impactful learning comes from courses that resonate with your work, challenges, and the goals you strive to achieve. This alignment between learning and doing not only enriches your professional journey but ensures that your efforts in certification lead to meaningful, tangible outcomes.

Identifying Available Resources

Diving deeper into the concept of utilising your immediate environment for skill acquisition, it's like unlocking a secret level in a game that's been available all along, yet remains unexplored. Your workplace isn't just a place to perform tasks and earn a paycheck; it's a dynamic learning ecosystem, ripe with opportunities for growth and development.

Consider the daily interactions with your colleagues. Every project, meeting, or casual conversation at the coffee machine can be a mini-masterclass in a specific skill or knowledge area. Your colleague, who excels at public speaking, the project manager with a knack for seamless team coordination, or the IT whiz who troubleshoots software issues with ease—all these individuals are potential mentors. The beauty of it? The learning is mutual. Just as you seek to absorb knowledge from them, there's something of value you can offer in return, fostering a culture of shared learning.

Why not initiate a 'skill swap' session within your team or department? It could be as simple as a short presentation over lunch, where team members share insights or tips related to their expertise. These sessions not only enhance skills but also boost team cohesion and morale.

Furthermore, pushing the boundaries of your regular duties to take on projects that stretch your capabilities can be incredibly rewarding. Volunteering for assignments that require a skill you're keen to develop serves a dual purpose: it shows initiative and drive, qualities prized by employers, and it provides a practical, hands-on learning experience that's far more impactful than any theoretical study.

In sum, the office landscape is more than just desks and computers—it's a vibrant community teeming with opportunities for those willing to seek them out. By adopting a proactive approach to learning, you transform everyday routines into exciting avenues for personal and professional growth. So, take a moment to look around and ask yourself, "What learning opportunities are hiding in plain sight?"

And here's a suggestion that might sound a bit radical—consider cutting down on the time you spend with OTT platforms like Netflix or endlessly scrolling through the news. The hours spent speculating about the next Prime Minister or getting lost in cricket updates are hours you could invest in yourself. Remember, every minute you spend absorbed in these distractions is a minute you're not learning, not growing.

So, take control of your resources, prioritise your learning, and watch as doors begin to open. Your journey of personal and professional development is just waiting for you to take that first step.

Value of learning

The workspace buzzes with untold stories of wisdom and expertise, often sitting quietly in the person next to you or the team across the hall. The value of learning from colleagues and subordinates is a treasure trove that's frequently overlooked, yet it's right there, within the everyday interactions and shared challenges.

Think about it—each person you work with brings a unique set of skills, experiences, and perspectives to the table. The fresh recruit might have a knack for the latest tech tools that could streamline your workflow. The colleague from another department could share insights into a project management tool that makes collaboration a breeze. And then there's the team member who's been with the company for decades, offering a wealth of institutional knowledge and historical context that no manual could ever provide.

Learning from those around you isn't just about acquiring new skills; it's about building a culture of shared knowledge and mutual respect. It turns the workplace into a dynamic classroom where everyone is both a teacher and a student. This kind of environment not only boosts individual competence but also enhances team cohesion and overall productivity.

So, how do you tap into this resource? Start with curiosity. Ask questions. Be genuinely interested in what others are doing and how they're doing it. Offer to share your own expertise in return. This exchange doesn't have to be formal—casual conversations over coffee, lunchtime learning sessions, or quick chats before a meeting can all be fertile ground for learning.

By valuing the knowledge and experience of your colleagues and subordinates, you not only enrich your own skill set but also contribute to creating a more inclusive and collaborative workplace culture. It's about recognizing that everyone, regardless of their position, has something valuable to teach and that learning is a collective journey.

Managing Time and Financial Investments

Starting a learning journey isn't just about wanting to grow – it's about reshuffling our daily routines and priorities. Smartly managing time and money can make the overwhelming seem achievable, especially when trying to fit learning into our busy schedules.

Here's the crux: it's about making choices that align with your goals. This might mean reassessing how you spend your downtime. For many of us, leisure activities—be it binge-watching TV series, scrolling through social media, or engaging in lengthy gaming sessions—eat up a significant chunk of our day. While relaxation is crucial for well-being, moderation is key. The trick is to find a balance that allows for both unwinding and personal development.

Start by taking a hard look at your typical day or week. Identify the pockets of time that could be reallocated to learning. Perhaps it's the hour after dinner you usually spend watching TV, or the half-hour each morning scrolling through your phone in bed. These moments, when redirected towards learning, can accumulate into substantial gains over time.

Financially, the principle is similar. Assess your spending on leisure and entertainment. Small adjustments, like opting for a more basic streaming service package or cutting back on frequent online shopping, can free up funds for courses, books, or other learning materials.

Remember, this doesn't mean stripping all joy and relaxation from your life. Instead, it's about prioritising activities that offer long-term benefits over those that offer only immediate gratification. Try to view learning not as a chore but as an enriching activity that's as deserving of your time and money as any leisure pursuit.

Practical steps like setting clear learning goals, creating a dedicated study schedule, and budgeting for educational investments can also help keep you on track. And don't forget to celebrate milestones along the way—this helps reinforce the value of your investments and keeps the motivation high.

Viewing fees as an investment

Understanding fees as investments rather than costs puts into perspective the long-term benefits of continuous learning. The investment in education, lasting perhaps fifteen years, sets the stage for benefits that grow throughout a forty-plus year career. By consistently updating and expanding your skills, you not only enhance your career stability but also increase the potential for higher returns in the form of promotions, new job opportunities, and the satisfaction that comes with personal achievement.

To navigate this investment-minded approach effectively:

Assess potential returns: Before enrolling in any program, consider how it aligns with your career goals and the potential benefits it could bring.

Allocate your budget with intention: Designate a portion of your income for personal and professional development, treating it as a critical component of your financial planning.

Seek out supportive funding, If not, don't stop, go for education loans. Good deals are out there. Better buy a Laptop, Tab or Kindle rather than an i-phone or fancy bike. Choice is yours. You want a smartphone or smarter you.

Measure the impact: Keep track of how each learning opportunity contributes to your growth. This will not only motivate you but also guide your future learning decisions.

By recognizing fees as strategic investments in your personal and professional development, you empower yourself to take charge of your growth trajectory. This approach not only positions you for immediate advancements but also lays a foundation for sustained success and fulfilment in your career.

Commitment to Learning

Learning new things and improving your skills is super important if you want to keep up with the world around you. Things change fast—new gadgets come out, the way we work changes, and what people need to know for their jobs can change too. That's why it's a good idea to keep learning new stuff on your own, even if no one is asking you to.

Think about it like this: the world isn't going to wait for anyone to catch up. So, if you want to stay in the game and not fall behind, you've got to take learning into your own hands. This means always being on the lookout for new things to learn that can help you at work or in life.

How can you do this? Start by figuring out what you want to get better at. It could be something that helps you at work, a new hobby, or just something you're curious about. Then, make a plan to learn it. You could spend a few hours every week watching value-adding videos online, reading and listening books, or trying out new things that help you learn.

Talking to people who know a lot about what you want to learn can help a lot too. This could be friends, family, or people you work with. They can give you advice, teach you new things, and help you see things in a different way. And sometimes, just talking about what you're learning can open up new chances for you to grow.

The bottom line is, learning new things is all about making a promise to yourself to keep getting better every day. It's about not standing still while everything else moves forward. So, get curious, make learning a regular part of your day, and enjoy seeing where it takes you.

Informed Decisions

When it comes to getting better at something, whether it's for your job or just because you're interested in it, it's super important to think carefully about how you use your time and money. These are your tools for learning, and using them wisely can really make a difference in how well you learn new skills.

Here's the deal: not all ways of learning are created equal. Some might be super expensive but not give you much back, while others could be almost free and teach you a ton. So, before you decide to spend your time or money on learning something new, take a step back and think about what you're really getting into. Ask yourself, "Is this the best way for me to learn this? Will this help me in the long run?"

Avoid searching for free tutorials or courses. You may come across online tutorials that align perfectly with your learning goals, saving you from investing in costly courses.. Or, you might decide that investing in a course is worth it because it gives you a deeper understanding or a certificate that helps your career.

Also, don't forget that learning isn't just about spending money. It's about spending your time well, too. We all have the same 24 hours in a day, so think about how you can use your time to learn something new in a way that fits your life. Maybe you listen to an educational podcast on your way to work, or spend half an hour reading about a new topic before bed.

In the end, the goal is to keep growing and getting better, using what you have in the best way possible.

This chapter has talked at length about how to do that, from choosing the right skills to learn, to finding resources and making learning a habit.

Remember, the path to learning new things is different for everyone. There's no one-size-fits-all answer. The key is to stay curious, be smart about how you use your resources, and keep pushing yourself to learn and grow. That's how you stay ahead of the game and make your mark on the world.

Chapter 4

Persistence

The Challenge of Sustained Effort

Initiating the process of learning a new skill typically comes with a high level of excitement. There's an undeniable surge of motivation when one decides to embark on this path. The selection of a particular skill, enrolling in a course, and even the act of payment represents significant first steps toward personal or professional development. This phase is characterized by a strong commitment and an eagerness to dive into new knowledge or competencies.

However, this initial enthusiasm often faces a gradual decline. The challenge isn't in the beginning but in sustaining the effort required to continue learning and growing. As time progresses, the excitement of the new venture can be overshadowed by the reality of the hard work and persistence needed. This shift from initial enthusiasm to the need for sustained effort is a pivotal point in the learning journey.

The ability to maintain momentum in the face of this reality separates those who achieve their learning objectives from those who fall short. It's a distinction that underscores the importance of persistence. Real growth and achievement come from the ongoing effort, from the commitment to continue learning even when it becomes challenging, and from the resilience to push through obstacles.

This transition from starting with enthusiasm to maintaining persistence encapsulates a common narrative in the pursuit of new skills or knowledge. It highlights the critical role of sustained effort and the need to embrace the long-term process of growth. The journey of learning, therefore, is not just about the excitement of beginning but also about the dedication and resilience required to continue, reflecting the broader theme of persistence as a cornerstone of personal and professional development.

Persistence after the initial commitment

Here's a perspective that might change the way we approach learning or any long-term goal: doing something difficult for a short period often seems more achievable than committing to even the simplest tasks over a longer stretch. For instance, hitting the gym hard for an hour a day for ten days might appear more doable than consistently exercising for twenty minutes daily over two years. Yet, it's the latter—those small, sustained efforts—that often lead to lasting change and success.

Short-term intensity and Long-term consistency

Short-term intensity often looks like a sprint. It's fueled by bursts of enthusiasm where you might dive deep into a subject or skill, putting in a lot of hours in a concentrated period. This approach can be useful for quick gains or meeting immediate goals.

Long-term consistency is more of a marathon. You need to keep making steady efforts over a while. It may not give quick big results, but it helps you understand things better, remember skills well, and become really good at it. Being consistent makes the skill a natural part of you, always there when you need it, instead of something you forget easily.

The real difference between people who succeed and those who don't comes down to this simple idea: it's often easier to work really hard for a short time than to keep doing even simple tasks over a long period.

Let's put it in plain words. When you try to do something challenging, but only for a little while, it feels doable because you know there's an end in sight. It's like running as fast as you can for a short distance. You can give it your all because you only have to keep it up for a short time.

But, if you're asked to keep doing something easy, yet you have to keep at it for a very long time, that's where it gets tough. It's like going for a morning walk for 30 minutes, and maintaining the routine for years together. The task - Walking, is not tough, but the continuity for months or years is the tougher part. The task itself isn't hard, but the need to keep doing it without giving up requires a lot of patience and determination.

In learning or getting better at anything, this principle holds true. Jumping in and working really hard for a few days might show quick results, but the real wins come from sticking with it day after day, even when the progress seems slow. That's how small efforts add up over time, leading to real improvement and success.

So, the message is clear: keep going, even when it feels too easy or too boring. It's those small, consistent efforts that make all the difference in the long run.

Strategies for Consistent Learning

Consistently maintaining a learning routine may appear challenging, yet with effective strategies in place, it is entirely achievable. Here are some tips to help you create a learning schedule that sticks and understand the importance of taking breaks.

Scheduled Learning Days

Allocating Monday, Tuesday, and Wednesday for focused learning sessions capitalizes on the fresh energy typically present at the beginning of the week. This period can be used to tackle new concepts, engage in deep study, or practice skills intensively. The key here is to set clear objectives for each session, ensuring that time is used efficiently and progress is made on specific learning goals.

Mid-Week Break

Taking Thursday off serves multiple purposes. It not only provides a mental break but also allows time for the information absorbed during the initial part of the week to settle. This rest period can enhance cognitive processes like memory consolidation, where the brain strengthens the newly learned information. During this break, engaging in activities unrelated to the learning topic—such as physical exercise, leisure reading, or hobbies—can rejuvenate the mind and body.

Resuming with Recharged Focus

Returning to learning on Friday and Saturday leverages the restorative effects of the break, allowing for renewed focus and energy. These days can be particularly effective for reinforcing the material covered earlier in the week, applying knowledge through practice, or exploring related areas of interest. The idea is to build upon the foundation laid in the first half of the week, solidifying understanding and skill.

Weekend Break

Concluding the week with a break on Sunday sets a rhythm that supports long-term sustainability. This day off before the start of a new week offers an opportunity for reflection—to assess progress, adjust goals, and plan for the upcoming week. It's also a time for mental rest, ensuring that you approach the new week with a clear mind and renewed motivation.

Making It Work for You

The effectiveness of this learning schedule hinges on personalization. Adjusting the schedule to fit personal preferences, work commitments, and lifestyle can enhance its sustainability. Some may find that alternative days' work better for their focused learning sessions, or that shorter, more frequent breaks align better with their concentration span.

Switching between focused learning and rest is based on knowing how the brain works. Balancing times of hard thinking with breaks helps avoid putting too much strain on the brain, improves remembering things, and keeps motivation strong for a long time.

Building something amazing doesn't happen all at once. It's like how the most famous landmarks around the world were made. They weren't just put there in one piece. They were built bit by bit. Take the Eiffel Tower, for example. It stands tall because of hundreds of tons of steel put together kilo by kilo, added up to a total of 7,000 metric tons. And think about this – it's held together by 2.5 million rivets, each one placed there by hand, one at a time. Even after being built, the Eiffel Tower doesn't just keep standing without care. Every seven years, it gets a new coat of paint.

This isn't just for looks; it's to keep it strong and sturdy, making sure it can stand tall for over a century.

So, if such a grand structure needs regular care to maintain its worth and stand tall, why wouldn't we? Just like the tower, our growth and learning are built step by step. Every little bit of new knowledge we pick up, every new skill we practise, adds up over time to make us better, stronger, and more capable. And just like the Eiffel Tower needs its regular touch-ups, we need to keep refreshing our skills and knowledge to stay sharp and valuable.

Learning and improving ourselves bit by bit not only helps us grow but also ensures that we can stand tall and proud, showing our true value to the world. It's about taking those small steps consistently, knowing that they all add up to something big in the end.

Optimising Conditions for Persistence

Sticking to an early morning routine for learning and personal growth is often more feasible than trying to fit these activities into a packed evening schedule. The simple reason? In the morning, the main obstacle to overcome is the comfort of your bed. Once you manage to get up, you've cleared the biggest hurdle.

Evenings, however, present a different story. After a day filled with work, navigating through traffic, and other responsibilities, the distractions multiply. There's the lure of TV, catching up on the news, social commitments, and conversations with friends or family. Each one competes for your attention, making it significantly harder to carve out a quiet moment for learning or self-improvement. The list of potential interruptions is long, and dodging all of them to focus on personal growth can feel like an uphill battle.

This contrast between morning and evening routines highlights a crucial point: by choosing to learn in the morning, you're not just picking a time slot. You're strategically placing your learning activities at a point in your day when you're less likely to be sidetracked by the myriad of distractions that accumulate by evening. This makes mornings an ideal time for those seeking to build a habit of persistent self-improvement, ensuring that personal growth activities don't get lost in the shuffle of daily life.

Incorporating learning into your mornings means you're leveraging a time when your willpower is fresh and distractions are minimal, setting a positive, proactive tone for the day ahead. This approach not only helps in sustaining a routine but also maximizes the effectiveness of the time you dedicate to learning and self-improvement.

Practical tips for consistent practice

Keeping up regular practice in anything is important but can be tough.To overcome challenges, you need a mix of planning and mental strength. Learn how to tackle common problems and see how staying focused can bring success and good results.

1. Set Clear, Achievable Goals

Start by defining clear, realistic goals. Break down larger objectives into smaller, manageable tasks. Achieving these smaller goals can provide a sense of progress and keep motivation high.

2. Establish a Routine

Consistency is easier to achieve when you have a set routine. Determine the best time of day for your practice and stick to it, making this activity a non-negotiable part of your day.

3. Create a Dedicated Space

Having a physical space dedicated to practice can help signal to your brain that it's time to focus. This space doesn't have to be large or elaborate, just consistently used for your practice sessions.

4. Minimize Distractions

Identify potential distractions in advance and take steps to minimize them. This might mean turning off your phone, using apps that block distracting websites, or practicing at a time when interruptions are less likely.

5. Use a Timer

Working with a timer can help keep practice sessions focused and productive. The Pomodoro Technique, which involves focused work for 25 minutes followed by a 5-minute break, can be particularly effective.

6. Seek Support

Share your goals with friends, family, or peers who can offer support and accountability. Sometimes, just knowing that someone else is cheering for you can provide an extra boost of motivation.

7. Accept Failure as Part of the Process

Understand that setbacks and failures are part of the learning process. Instead of getting discouraged, analyze what went wrong and how you can adjust your approach moving forward.

8. Celebrate Progress

Take time to acknowledge and celebrate your achievements, no matter how small. Recognizing your progress can reinforce your commitment and enhance your self-confidence.

Determination and Success

Accepting these practical tips with strong determination and focus can lead to big achievements. Overcoming challenges and reaching your goals boosts self-confidence significantly. This confidence can inspire you to tackle other goals you've been delaying. Each success adds to the last one, creating a cycle of positive results and personal growth.

Remember, the journey to mastering a skill or achieving a goal is not just about the end goal but about the growth and learning along the way. Your determination and the strategies you use for consistency play a crucial role in success, making your experience fulfilling and rewarding.

Personal Reflections on Learning

After thirty years in my job, when I was fifty, I decided to try something new. I signed up for a six-month online class on Digital Transformation from a well-known university in the US. I found this course through Simplilearn. It required me to be online for four hours every weekend, from 7 pm to 11 pm, with just a short ten-minute break for dinner.

In this class, most people knew a lot about IT, which was different from my background in manufacturing. This meant I had to work twice as hard. Not only was I trying to understand the main ideas of the course, but I was also learning new terms in IT at the same time.

But I stuck with it. I finished the course, got my certificate, and felt really good about what I had achieved. This success was a big deal for me. It showed me that I could learn new things and keep up, even if it was a bit tough at first.

Encouraged by finishing this course, I didn't stop there. Two months later, I signed up for another course to become a Certified Auditor for Industry 4.0, offered by TUV-SUD+CII.

This experience of learning new skills at this point in my career taught me a lot. Most importantly, I saw how sticking with something, even when it's hard, can really pay off. It made me feel more confident and ready to tackle other goals that I had been putting off.

Jumping from my recent adventures in learning to the broader journey has been an eye-opener. Through both the successes and the setbacks of diving into various courses, I've gathered a handful of key lessons that have reshaped my approach to learning and tackling new challenges.

Accepting Failure as a Stepping Stone

One of the biggest lessons came from the times things didn't go as planned. Every course I attempted wasn't a straight path to success. There were moments of confusion, times when I couldn't keep up, and even instances where I questioned if I had made the right choice. But each setback taught me something valuable. I learned that failure isn't the opposite of success; it's part of the journey to achieving it. Each misstep was a lesson in disguise, showing me where I needed to focus more and reminding me that persistence pays off.

The Power of Adaptability

Being open to change and willing to adjust my learning methods when necessary helped me overcome these hurdles. This flexibility was crucial in allowing me to absorb new information more effectively and apply it to my goals.

The Importance of a Support System

Another key takeaway was the importance of having a support system. Learning, especially in areas outside your comfort zone, can feel isolating at times. However, reaching out to instructors, participating in forums, and even sharing my struggles and triumphs with friends and family made a huge difference. These connections not only provided moral support but often offered different perspectives and solutions to the challenges I faced.

The Ripple Effect of Persistence

Persisting through my learning journey, I decided to tackle the Independent Director Test conducted by the Indian Institute of Corporate Affairs (IICA) under the Ministry of Corporate Affairs (MCA). My dedication paid off when I passed and got certified on my first attempt. This success was not just about adding another qualification to my profile; it was a testament to the power of persistence and choosing goals that aligned with my interests and strengths.

However, not every step of this journey was smooth. I enrolled in a Supply Chain Management course from IIT, only to find that the subject matter didn't resonate with me, and the complexity of the content was challenging. Despite my best efforts, I had to make the tough decision to drop out halfway through. This experience was a stark reminder that not every learning attempt fits our path or capabilities, sometimes referred to as an "inorganic" attempt. Yet, this setback didn't dampen my enthusiasm for learning. Instead, I redirected my energy and completed a course in Accounting & Financing from Udemy. This course, more in line with my abilities and interests, reinforced the idea that learning is a personal journey, and success comes from finding the right fit for our unique learning styles and goals.

The journey underscored a crucial insight: the key to climbing the ladder of skills and personal development isn't necessarily a higher IQ (Intelligence Quotient). Instead, it's about nurturing an improved EQ (Emotional Quotient). Emotional intelligence, the ability to understand and manage our emotions and those of others, plays a pivotal role in overcoming setbacks, adapting to new challenges, and persisting in the face of adversity.

This blend of successes and challenges taught me that persistence in learning isn't just about stubbornly pushing forward. It's about adapting to setbacks, understanding our strengths and weaknesses, and continuously seeking opportunities for growth that align with our capabilities and interests. Each step, whether a stride forward or a momentary stumble, contributes to our overall growth and the expansive ripple effect of persistent learning.

For Example,

Karoly Takacs is an inspiring figure in the world of sports, renowned for his remarkable comeback in shooting after a life-altering injury. Takacs was a member of the Hungarian Army and a world-class shooter, aiming for the Olympics. His life changed dramatically in 1938 when a grenade blew up in his right hand, the hand he used for shooting. Most people might have given up their dreams after such a severe injury, but not Takacs. He didn't let the world know what he was up to; instead, he quietly started teaching himself to shoot with his left hand.

After a year of secret practice, he surprised everyone by showing up at the Hungarian National Shooting Championships. It wasn't just a symbolic gesture; he competed and won, beating all the other shooters who were using their dominant hands. But Takacs didn't stop there. His greatest moments came when he won Olympic gold medals for rapid-fire pistol shooting in both the 1948 London Olympics and the 1952 Helsinki Olympics.

Each medal was a testament to his incredible perseverance and willpower. Imagine the strength it took to start from scratch with his non-dominant hand and go on to achieve what most able-bodied shooters only dream of. Takacs's story is not just about sports; it's a powerful reminder of human potential and the ability to overcome adversity with determination and hard work. It shows that real limitations are only those we set in our minds, and with enough persistence, we can redefine what's possible.

Accepting Your Flaws and Moving Forward

Learning to appreciate yourself just as you are is crucial. It's about acknowledging all parts of you—the good and the areas for improvement—and accepting them. This approach builds self-confidence and lessens the concern over others' opinions. Remember, you have the full right to be wrong.

Don't imagine yourself in a witness box, bombarding yourself with questions about why you didn't achieve something or why something went wrong. This way of thinking keeps you stuck in a cycle of negativity, preventing you from enjoying the present and moving forward.

Constantly criticizing yourself for past mistakes or things you wish you'd done differently can have serious effects on your mental and emotional health. It's like carrying around a heavy backpack filled with "what ifs" and "if onlys" that weighs you down. This self-prosecution keeps your focus on what went wrong, instead of what you can do right now to move forward.

When you dwell on past regrets, it's like watching the same movie of your life's mistakes on repeat, without ever getting to change the ending. This can lead to feelings of sadness, anxiety, and even depression, because it feels like you're stuck in a loop of negativity. It also stops you from seeing the opportunities for growth and learning that are right in front of you.

Living in the past and punishing yourself for it means you're not living in the present. You miss out on the joy of the moment and the chance to make new, happier memories. It can also hurt your relationships with others, as it's hard for people to connect with someone who's always looking backward, not at what's happening now.

Instead, try to shift towards self-acceptance. Recognize that dwelling on past regrets or non-achievements isn't productive. It's not about forgetting these experiences but rather learning from them without letting them define your entire being. Moving from being your biggest critic to being your own supporter can significantly change how you feel about yourself and what you can accomplish in life. Be your own scaffolding, rise on it. Remember, every person has areas they excel in and areas where they face challenges.

The key to moving past this is to start forgiving yourself. Understand that everyone makes mistakes, and it's part of being human. Instead of asking "Why did I do that?" start asking "What can I learn from this?" This shift in perspective opens up a path to healing and growth, allowing you to leave the heavy backpack of regrets behind and start a new journey with a lighter load.

The Illusion of Perfection

Trying to be perfect all the time is like chasing something that doesn't really exist. It's like running after a finish line that keeps moving farther away, no matter how fast you run. This can make you feel tired and upset because it seems like you're never good enough. Instead, it's better to focus on getting better bit by bit. This means looking at the small ways you can improve every day, rather than trying to be flawless.

Perfection is a tricky idea because it suggests there's a point where you can't get any better. But in real life, there's always something new to learn or a way to grow. Progress, or getting better over time, is more about the journey. It includes trying, making mistakes, and learning from them. When you learn from mistakes, it is called failing forward, if you regret it is called failing backward. Choice is yours.

When you care more about making progress than being perfect, you take the pressure off yourself. It becomes okay to try things and not get them right the first time. This way of thinking helps you keep going, even when things get tough, because you see mistakes as chances to learn, not as failures.

Choosing progress over perfection is not about giving up on doing well. It's about setting realistic goals and appreciating the hard work it takes to reach them. This change can make you happier and less stressed because it fits better with how life really works.

Why striving for continuous improvement is more beneficial than seeking perfection

Striving for continuous improvement is like choosing a path that always leads you to new discoveries about yourself and what you can do. It's better than trying to be perfect because perfection is like a fixed point that doesn't really exist. You can never reach it, and trying to can make you feel stuck or unhappy.

When you focus on getting better a little bit at a time, you're always moving forward. You learn from what didn't work and use that knowledge to do better next time. This approach is great because it means you're always growing and changing. You're not afraid to try new things or take risks, because you know that's how you learn.

Improving bit by bit also makes you more flexible and ready to handle whatever comes your way. Instead of worrying about making mistakes, you see them as part of the process. This makes life a lot less stressful and more enjoyable.

In the end, aiming for continuous improvement lets you achieve more than you might have thought possible. It's about enjoying the journey, not just waiting to reach some perfect destination that doesn't exist. This way, you get to celebrate every small win and see how far you've come, which is a great feeling.

For Example,

Rovio, the company behind Angry Birds, didn't hit success straight away. They actually made 51 games before Angry Birds, and none of those games became big hits. But they didn't stop trying. With each new game, they learned something - what players liked, what they didn't, and what made a game fun.

When they made Angry Birds, their 52nd game, they used everything they learned from the past. Angry Birds was easy to play, had cute characters, and challenges that made people want to keep playing. This game became super popular all over the world.

Their story shows us that if you keep working hard and don't give up, you can achieve your goals. It also shows how important it is to learn from your mistakes. Rovio didn't see their first 51 games as failures. Instead, they saw them as steps to get better and make something people would love.

Just like Rovio learned from their earlier attempts before creating Angry Birds, J.K. Rowling's story with Harry Potter is another inspiring example. Before Harry Potter became a global phenomenon, Rowling faced her own set of challenges. She sent her manuscript to 12 publishers, and all of them said no. They didn't think Harry Potter would be a success. But Rowling didn't give up. She believed in her story and her characters.

Finally, Bloomsbury Publishing decided to give Harry Potter a chance. They published her book, and the rest, as they say, is history. Harry Potter became one of the most beloved series in the world, turning into movies, games, and even theme parks.

Rowling's journey reminds us that rejection is not the end. It's part of the process. She kept pushing forward, believing in her work, even when others didn't see its value. This teaches us to believe in ourselves and our dreams, even when faced with setbacks.

Both Rovio and J.K. Rowling shows that success often comes after many tries and rejections. They teach us the power of persistence, learning from feedback, and never giving up on what we believe in. Their stories encourage us to keep going, learn from every step, and stay true to our visions.,

Self-Forgiveness: Forgiving ourselves for past mistakes and misdeeds is a crucial step towards finding inner peace and moving forward in a healthier, more positive way. Here are some steps that can guide you on the path to self-forgiveness:

Acknowledge and Accept: Recognize the mistake or misdeed openly. Acceptance is the first step towards healing. It's important to understand that acknowledging your fault doesn't mean you are a bad person; it means you are human and capable of growth.

Understand the Why: Spend some time reflecting on what led you to make those choices. Understanding the reasons behind your actions can help prevent similar mistakes in the future and can offer insights into your values and motivations.

Learn from the Experience: Every mistake is a learning opportunity. Ask yourself what you can take away from this experience. How has it shaped your understanding, and what can you do differently moving forward?

Make Amends if Possible: If your actions have hurt others, consider making amends in a way that is healthy and constructive. This could be an apology, a gesture to show you've changed, or other actions to rectify the situation, if possible.

Release the Guilt: Holding onto guilt and regret can be harmful to your mental health. Find ways to let go of these negative feelings. This might involve writing a letter to yourself, talking it out with a trusted friend, or practicing mindfulness and meditation to help release these emotions.

Practice Self-Compassion: Be kind to yourself. Understand that everyone makes mistakes and that they don't define your worth as a person. Treat yourself with the same kindness and understanding that you would offer a friend in a similar situation.

Move Forward with a Positive Action: Channel your feelings into positive actions. Use what you've learned to better yourself and your community. This could mean volunteering, helping others avoid similar mistakes, or simply committing to being a more mindful and kinder person.

Seek Support: Sometimes, we need help from others to truly forgive ourselves. This could be a therapist, a support group, or friends and family. Don't hesitate to reach out for the support you need to move past your mistakes.

When you learn to forgive yourself, it's as if you're taking a heavy weight off your shoulders, allowing you to stand up straighter and walk more freely into the future.

This process is deeply personal and incredibly important because it touches on the very core of who we are. It's about recognizing that, yes, you've made mistakes—just like everyone else—but these don't define your entire being. Self-forgiveness opens up a space for kindness and understanding within yourself that perhaps wasn't there before.

In terms of personal growth, forgiving yourself is a turning point. It marks the moment you decide to stop being your own worst critic and start being your own supporter. This shift in perspective fuels your desire to improve, learn, and grow because you know you're worthy of your own efforts and dreams.

For your mental health, the impact of self-forgiveness is profound. It's linked to lower levels of depression, anxiety, and stress. *Why?* Because it replaces negative self-talk with a more compassionate inner dialogue. Imagine having a friend inside your head who understands and supports you, rather than one who constantly reminds you of your faults. That's what self-forgiveness can do.

Remember, you're not alone in this. Everyone has something they wish they could do over, but not everyone realizes the power of self-forgiveness in moving past these regrets. It's a journey, and like all journeys, it can have its rough patches. But also like all journeys, it can lead to beautiful destinations—increased self-awareness, more meaningful relationships, and a deeper sense of peace. You're taking steps towards becoming not just who you are but who you want to be. And that's something truly special.

Overcoming the Need for External Validation

Remember, you don't need to seek approval or validation from others to know your worth. Other people aren't in a position to judge you, so it's important not to give them the power to assess you and decide if you're doing well or not.

When you stop looking for others to acknowledge your achievements or your choices, you start to take back control of your own self-esteem and confidence. It's about trusting yourself and your judgment. Just because someone else doesn't see your value doesn't mean it's not there. You know your journey, your struggles, and your victories better than anyone else.

Instead of waiting for someone else to give you a "thumbs up," give it to yourself. Celebrate your own successes, no matter how small they might seem. By doing this, you build a sense of self that's based on your own standards and achievements, not on what others think.

The shift away from this need starts with recognizing your own value. It's about getting to know yourself—your strengths, your weaknesses, and everything in between—and accepting all parts of you.

Building this kind of self-reliance involves a few steps. First, start by setting your own standards for success. What matters to you? What makes you feel fulfilled? By defining these for yourself, you create a sense of internal validation that no one can take away.

Next, practice mindfulness and self-reflection. Pay attention to times when you're seeking validation and ask yourself why. What are you hoping to gain, and is there a way you can give that to yourself? Often, we look for external validation when we're feeling insecure or unsure. Recognizing these moments can help you address the underlying needs.

Lastly, surround yourself with people who support your journey to self-validation. This doesn't mean they always agree with you, but they respect your right to make your own choices and believe in your own worth. These relationships can be a powerful source of support as you learn to validate yourself.

Focusing on Yourself

Focusing on winning over others can lead to a constant cycle of comparison and competition, which might not always result in personal growth or happiness. Instead, shifting your focus towards self-improvement every day can be a more fulfilling and effective goal. Aim to enhance yourself by just a little bit every day, whether that's learning something new, developing a skill, or making a small change towards a healthier lifestyle.

This approach of aiming for incremental improvement is about acknowledging that growth is a journey, not a race against others. It's about setting personal milestones and celebrating your own progress, no matter how small it might seem. Each small step forward accumulates over time, leading to significant changes and developments in your abilities, knowledge, and overall well-being.

By concentrating on improving yourself, you cultivate a mindset of self-reflection and continuous learning. This mindset not only helps you become more adaptable and resilient in the face of challenges but also fosters a sense of satisfaction and accomplishment that comes from within, not from external validation or comparison with others.

Remember, the goal is not to be better than anyone else, but to be better than you were yesterday. This perspective encourages a positive, growth-focused approach to life, where the only person you're truly trying to surpass is the person you were the day before.

Being human

Being human comes with a range of emotions, and it's completely normal to have moments when you feel down or discouraged. What's important is how you respond to these feelings. Bouncing back and facing challenges head-on is a crucial part of personal growth and resilience.

When you're feeling low, it's an opportunity to pause and reflect on what's causing those feelings. Sometimes, it's a sign that you need to take care of yourself, maybe by resting or spending time on activities that bring you joy. Other times, it might be a signal that something in your life needs to change.

Bouncing back doesn't mean ignoring your feelings or pretending everything is fine. It means acknowledging how you feel, giving yourself time to process those emotions, and then gradually finding ways to move forward. This could involve setting small, manageable goals to help regain your confidence, seeking support from friends or family, or finding motivation in the challenges themselves.

Taking on challenges head-on is about embracing the opportunity to grow and learn from difficult situations. It's about seeing obstacles not just as barriers to your goals, but as chances to become stronger and more skilled. Each challenge you face and overcome adds to your experience and resilience, making you better prepared for whatever comes next.

It's okay to seek help when you need it, whether that's talking to someone you trust, joining a support group, or seeking professional advice. *You're not alone, and reaching out for support is a sign of strength, not weakness.*

"Wherever you may be, whatever you may be, if you are willing to strive, you can evolve yourself beyond the limitations of nature."

– Sadhguru

Chapter 5

Emotional Quotient

Emotional Quotient (EQ) is all about understanding and managing our feelings in a positive way to reduce stress, communicate well, connect with others, tackle problems, and solve conflicts. It helps us build better relationships, do well in school and work, and reach our goals. While IQ stays the same, EQ can get better with practice and focus.

Having a high emotional intelligence (EQ) is vital for attaining top positions, surpassing even IQ. While a high IQ is beneficial in academic and professional settings, EQ plays a pivotal role in managing stress and emotions effectively in senior positions. Leaders who possess robust emotional intelligence can regulate their own emotions to enhance decision-making and empathise with others to foster better teamwork and leadership.

EQ is about our ability to recognize, understand, and manage our own emotions and the emotions of others. It involves

★ **Self-awareness:** Recognizing your own emotions and their effect on your thoughts and behavior.

★ **Self-regulation:** Being able to control or redirect disruptive emotions and impulses.

- ★ **Motivation:** Harnessing emotions to pursue goals with energy and persistence.
- ★ **Empathy:** Understanding the emotional makeup of other people.
- ★ **Social skills:** Managing relationships to move people in desired directions.

Improving your EQ can lead to better stress management, improved communication skills, and stronger relationships. Unlike IQ, EQ can be developed and enhanced over time with conscious effort and practice. For example, practicing mindfulness and empathy can help enhance one's emotional intelligence.

Intelligence Quotient

IQ, on the other hand, is a measure of a person's intellectual abilities compared to the average population. It includes

- ★ **Analytical thinking:** The ability to solve problems using logic and reasoning.
- ★ **Memory:** The capacity to remember information.
- ★ **Mathematical ability:** How well a person can solve mathematical problems.
- ★ **Understanding of language:** Comprehension and use of language.

IQ is often considered to be less malleable than EQ. It's measured through standardized tests and is thought to be influenced by genetics, though the environment also plays a role in its development. A high IQ can lead to academic success and is often valued in fields that require a lot of analytical processing and problem-solving skills.

Shifting focus from activities that don't add value to ones that do is a journey that hinges significantly on one's

Emotional Quotient (EQ). Unlike Intelligence Quotient (IQ), which is largely considered static throughout a person's life, EQ stands out for its capacity for growth and improvement. This adaptability of EQ underscores its vital role in personal and professional development, especially in leadership roles.

Research and observations have consistently shown that top positions are often held by individuals with high EQ rather than just high IQ. The reason behind this trend is that emotional intelligence encompasses a range of skills crucial for leadership, including empathy, self-awareness, and the ability to navigate complex social situations. These skills enable leaders to motivate their teams, resolve conflicts effectively, and create a positive work environment, which are key components of successful leadership.

Moreover, the journey to the top involves making strategic decisions about where to direct one's efforts. It's not always about moving faster but moving smarter. Choosing the right direction over merely speeding up emphasises the importance of strategic thinking—a hallmark of high EQ. Even a minor shift in direction, as slight as one degree, can significantly alter one's trajectory towards a more intentional and fulfilling destination. This ability to pivot, to reassess, and realign one's course, is invaluable in both personal growth and career advancement.

Changing your focus doesn't have to be a big deal. It can begin with small, intentional steps taken gradually. This is especially important when working on your emotional intelligence. Unlike a long journey, changing focus can happen in an instant, paving the way for a path that aligns with your values and goals.

Improving emotional intelligence, rather than just IQ, is key for leadership and personal growth. It helps you let go of unproductive tasks and focus on what matters, guiding you towards success and satisfaction. This flexibility and focus on growth show how emotional intelligence can lead to achieving top positions and reaching your full potential.

Stepping Out of Comfort Zones

Leaving your comfort zone behind and moving steadfastly towards what you truly believe in is a vital step in personal and professional growth. It's crucial to understand that living comfortably and holding strong to your convictions rarely coexist without conflict. This dichotomy between conviction and convenience is akin to trying to house two opposing forces under one roof—it simply doesn't work.

The journey to personal growth is not about escaping physical barriers but rather breaking free from the self-imposed limitations of comfort and the habit of making excuses. Achieving this liberation requires something akin to 'escape velocity'—a force strong enough to propel you beyond the gravitational pull of your existing habits and fears. Just like a rocket needs significant thrust to break free from Earth's gravity and embark on its journey to space, you need a powerful push to step beyond the familiar and embrace the challenges that lead to growth. Once this initial barrier is overcome, reaching your 'moon'—your goals and dreams—becomes a matter of consistent effort and direction.

Enhancing your emotional intelligence, or EQ, is an essential part of this process. However, becoming emotionally stronger doesn't necessitate burying yourself in academic texts on emotional intelligence or seeking out specialists. For most people, the path to improving EQ involves practical, everyday actions that are both simple and achievable. It's about making deliberate choices to understand and manage your emotions more effectively, developing empathy for others, and strengthening your social skills—skills that are crucial for navigating life's challenges and building meaningful relationships.

It's a process of breaking free from the 'gravity' of your current state, powered by the conviction to grow and improve. By focusing on actionable steps to enhance your EQ, you prepare yourself to handle whatever challenges come your way, ultimately leading to a richer, more fulfilling life.

Practical Steps to Enhance EQ

Improving your Emotional Quotient (EQ) doesn't have to be complicated, involves deep dives into heavy books, or expensive sessions with consultants. You can enhance your EQ through straightforward, practical steps that are easy to integrate into your daily life. Here's how:

Listen Actively: Start by really listening when others talk, not just waiting for your turn to speak. Pay attention to their words, tone, and body language. This helps in understanding others' perspectives and emotions better.

Reflect on Your Emotions: Spend some time each day reflecting on how you felt throughout the day. Try to understand why you felt a certain way in different situations. This practice can increase your self-awareness, a core component of EQ.

Practice Empathy: Try to put yourself in someone else's shoes. When someone shares something with you, think about how they might be feeling. Ask yourself, "How would I feel in their situation?" This can help build your empathy muscle.

Manage Stress Effectively: Learn stress management techniques that work for you, whether it's deep breathing, meditation, exercise, or a hobby. Managing your stress well can prevent it from affecting your emotions and reactions.

Improve Communication Skills: Work on clear and effective communication. This includes not just how you convey messages but also how you interpret others' messages and respond to them. Good communication is key to better relationships and understanding.

Seek Feedback: Don't be afraid to ask for feedback on your interactions and how you handle emotions. Feedback from trusted friends, family, or colleagues can offer insights into areas you might need to work on.

Practice Gratitude: Regularly acknowledging what you're thankful for can shift your focus from negative to positive, improving your outlook and interactions with others.

Resolve Conflicts Thoughtfully: When disagreements arise, approach them with a calm and open mind. Focus on finding solutions rather than winning the argument. This can help in developing better problem-solving skills and maintaining positive relationships.

Each of these steps can lead to significant improvements in your EQ over time. They don't require grand gestures or dramatic changes in your routine—just small, consistent efforts to be more mindful of your and others' emotions. By integrating these practices into your daily life, you can enhance your emotional intelligence, leading to better personal and professional relationships and a more fulfilling life.

Improving Emotional Quotient (EQ) is a journey that unfolds behind the scenes, deeply intertwined with our daily habits, actions, and behaviors. These everyday practices act as the frontline in our quest to enhance our emotional intelligence.

Consider the process of updating your habits as akin to the natural process of losing old teeth to make room for new, stronger ones. Each old habit you shed paves the way for a new, more beneficial practice. For instance, if you decide to stop buying newspapers, a seemingly small choice, you're essentially taking a step towards strengthening your emotional intelligence. This decision not only reduces the intake of potentially distressing news but also frees up time. This time can then be redirected towards activities that foster growth, such as reading books that enhance your skills or knowledge.

This metaphor of shedding teeth symbolises the gradual process of transformation. As you replace non-productive habits with fruitful ones, your 'emotional muscle' becomes stronger day by day. This ongoing refinement of habits nudges the needle of your EQ meter from red, through yellow, and into the green zone—showing good emotional skills. Unlike a speedometer in a car or bike, this EQ meter measures emotional depth and understanding, not speed.

Establishing specific goals with deadlines is crucial to prevent procrastination and ensure timely task completion. Linking objectives to timelines creates a framework that encourages action and cultivates discipline, both pivotal for enhancing emotional intelligence (EQ).

Enhancing EQ involves subtly reshaping daily practices, demonstrating the impact of incremental change. Even minor adjustments in habits can result in significant shifts in emotional intelligence. This journey, characterised by patience and perseverance, enhances emotional strength for navigating life's challenges effectively.

Incorporating Discipline

Incorporating discipline into our lives, especially when it comes to emotional growth and learning new skills, involves setting clear goals with specific deadlines. This structured approach helps combat procrastination, a common barrier to progress. By defining what we want to achieve and when we aim to achieve it, we create a sense of urgency and accountability. This not only clarifies our priorities but also provides a roadmap to follow, making it easier to stay on track and measure progress.

The act of setting goals and deadlines does more than just keep procrastination at bay; it also fosters a mindset geared towards action and achievement. This discipline extends beyond merely completing tasks—it cultivates an ability to make decisions more quickly and confidently. In doing so, we become more agile in our responses to challenges and opportunities.

Moreover, this approach encourages us to shed any guilt associated with past procrastination or unachieved goals. Instead of dwelling on what hasn't been done, we focus on actionable steps forward. Embracing new activities becomes less daunting, as the disciplined framework we've established allows for exploration and growth without the fear of losing direction.

The benefits of this disciplined approach are manifold. It enhances our ability to adapt, making us more resilient in the face of change. We learn to embrace new experiences with enthusiasm rather than hesitation, enriching our personal and professional lives. Discipline, therefore, is not just about adhering to a schedule; it's about evolving into more versatile, competent individuals who are equipped to navigate the complexities of life with confidence and grace.

As you practice setting clear goals and adhering to deadlines, you'll find your ability to switch tasks becomes more fluid and quicker. This improvement comes from dropping the guilt you've been carrying about past delays or failures. Now lighter and nimbler, you're ready to tackle what comes next with greater ease and less delay.

Additionally, the simple act of keeping a pen and paper close by transforms your ability to hold onto fleeting thoughts. Ideas can come and go in a flash, and without a method to capture them, they're likely gone for good. By writing down your thoughts as soon as they arise, you prevent them from disappearing. This method doesn't just preserve your ideas; it organizes them, making it straightforward to prioritize and act upon them later. This approach aligns with your disciplined strategy, ensuring that your newfound clarity and direction are backed up by a practical system for noting and acting on your insights.

These methods not only make you more efficient and ready for change but also keep you progressing steadily, free from the setbacks of before, and equipped with an effective way to manage your ideas. Adopting this disciplined strategy, complemented by tangible steps for capturing your thoughts, sets a strong base for ongoing personal and professional development.

Seeking and Offering Help

Improving your EQ, or how well you understand and handle emotions, is important for getting along with others and doing well in most jobs. It's about learning and getting better at dealing with people and your feelings. One big part of this is being okay with asking for help and also giving a hand to others when they need it. When you're not too proud to ask for advice, it shows you're willing to learn and grow. This makes it easier for others to come up to you, share ideas, and help each other out.

Let's say you're working on something tough and you realize you're stuck. Instead of just spinning your wheels, you reach out to a coworker or a friend. This does a couple of things. First, it shows you're serious about getting better, not just looking smart all the time. Second, it makes the people you ask feel good because you value their knowledge. And usually, they're more than happy to share what they know.

But it's not just about getting help; it's also about giving it. When someone else is in a tight spot and you lend them a hand, it builds trust and strengthens your relationship with them. This back-and-forth of giving and receiving help can make everyone involved better at handling emotions and working together.

This whole thing—asking for help when you need it and offering it when someone else does—is a big part of growing your emotional smarts. It's like building a network where everyone supports each other, making the whole group stronger and more connected. So, don't be shy about asking for help or stepping up to assist others. It's one of the best ways to improve how you deal with emotions and interact with people around you.

Listening carefully to others is just as key to boosting your EQ. Real listening is more than catching words that come out of someone's mouth; it's about connecting with what they're sharing from their perspective. This kind of active listening isn't only about improving how you talk with people; it's about becoming more patient and, by extension, growing your emotional intelligence. When you listen with the goal to truly understand, not just to reply, you pick up on feelings and thoughts of others that you might miss otherwise. This understanding is crucial for developing your emotional smarts.

Paying attention in this way and being patient shows a lot about you, too. It teaches you empathy—how to feel what others feel—and helps you get better at seeing things from someone else's point of view. These skills have a big effect on how you connect with people and understand them better.

All in all, improving your EQ really benefits from being willing to ask for help and just as ready to give it. Taking part in these actions sets the stage for getting to know yourself and others more deeply. It creates a space where everyone is encouraged to grow and support one another.

"Anything is possible if you believe in yourself."
– BK Shivani

Chapter 6

Change Your Orbit

Everyone tends to fall into a set routine, engaging in nearly identical activities day after day, year after year. This consistent pattern of behavior, this well-trodden path we adhere to, is what can be termed our "orbit." It's a concept that explains how our daily practices and comfort zones shape the trajectory of our lives, often without us even realizing it. People who share the same orbit, or life path, typically exhibit similar habits and, as a result, often see similar outcomes in their lives.

This notion of life orbits offers a lens through which we can view our actions and their repercussions. It highlights the importance of our daily routines and comfort zones in determining the direction our lives take. When we stick to what's familiar, choosing not to venture beyond the confines of our established orbit, we limit our experiences and opportunities for growth. This sameness in our actions leads to a sameness in our outcomes, making it difficult to achieve different or more ambitious goals.

However, the realization that we are following a predetermined orbit isn't meant to discourage us. Rather, it serves as a wake-up call, an invitation to assess the path we're on. It challenges us to consider whether our current orbit aligns with our aspirations and, if not, to take deliberate steps toward changing it. This might involve altering our daily routines, stepping out of our comfort zones, and adopting new habits that propel us toward the outcomes we desire.

The concept also dismantles the notion that luck is the primary driver of success. Instead, it emphasizes the power of our actions and choices. Those who find themselves in higher orbits, achieving greater success, don't get there through sheer chance. They reach these heights by intentionally modifying their habits and behaviors, and accepting opportunities for personal and professional development.

In essence, our orbits are not fixed. They are fluid and can be altered with conscious effort and a willingness to embrace change. Recognizing the orbit we're in is merely the first step. The real work lies in deciding to accepting on a new trajectory—one that challenges us, enriches our experiences, and leads to more fulfilling outcomes. This journey of orbit change is not just about achieving different results; it's about transforming who we are and how we navigate the world around us.

For Example,

A.M. Naik, the Chairman Emeritus of Larsen & Toubro Limited. Naik's story is one of remarkable transformation. He didn't settle for the ordinary.

Starting off, Naik's journey wasn't destined for the top of a construction giant. He began humbly, as a junior engineer. But he didn't let his beginnings define him. Instead, he set his sights higher.

Naik saw opportunities where others saw obstacles. He climbed the ladder within Larsen & Toubro Limited, taking on challenges and responsibilities as they came. He didn't shy away from the tough tasks; he tackled them head-on.

Over time, Naik's efforts paid off. He steered the company through turbulent times, demonstrating resilience and vision. He didn't just lead; he inspired.

Under his leadership, Larsen & Toubro Limited expanded its horizons, venturing into new sectors and markets. Naik's strategic decisions propelled the company to new heights, solidifying its position as a key player in the industry.

Naik's journey is a testament to the power of perseverance and determination. He didn't let his background limit his aspirations. Instead, he redefined his trajectory, leaving a lasting legacy in the business world.

Myth of Luck

First, let's address the myth of luck. Luck might seem like the reason behind someone's sudden rise or achievement, but when you look closer, you'll often find a pattern of hard work, smart decisions, and a willingness to step out of your comfort zone. These individuals make choices every day that align with their goals, even when those choices require sacrifice or are uncomfortable.

It's a common belief that luck plays a major role in someone's success. However, this overlooks the real factors behind achieving high positions and making significant life changes. People who find themselves in "higher orbits" - those leading more successful, fulfilling lives - often share certain habits that distinguish them from others.

In their personal time, they engage in activities that add value to their lives and careers, rather than defaulting to passive entertainment or distractions. This might involve reading books that expand their understanding, practicing mindfulness to enhance self-awareness, or dedicating time to hobbies that improve their mental health and creativity.

These "behind the curtains" efforts are crucial to their advancement. It's not just about what you see in public—the speeches, the accolades, or the successes. It's about the hours of learning, the moments of self-reflection, the discipline in maintaining healthy habits, and the commitment to continuous self-improvement. This dedicated personal time is spent on activities that directly contribute to their growth, pushing them further into higher orbits.

This understanding challenges the notion of luck as the primary driver of success. Instead, it highlights the importance of deliberate practice, and the pursuit of activities that genuinely contribute to personal and professional development.

Luck isn't the key; it's about your hard work and progress.

The Process of Orbit Change

If you're on a path that's pretty much a circle. You're moving, sure, but you're not getting closer to where you want to be. To change that, first, you need persistence. It's like deciding to take a step off the familiar path. It might seem scary or hard, but the more you keep at it, the more you realize you can venture further and make your path.

Next up is upskilling. This is about adding new tools to your toolbox. If you've been walking all this time, learning a new skill is like getting a bike. Suddenly, you can go faster and reach places that seemed too far before. It's about making yourself more capable and versatile.

Then there's the aspect of understanding ourselves and interacting with others. This is crucial because it's not just about what you can do; it's also about how you connect with people and your own self-awareness. Improving in this area is like acquiring a map and compass for your personal journey. While you might have the means to move forward faster, now you also know where you're going and how to navigate the complexities of life. It enhances your awareness of your surroundings, strengthens your connections with others, and improves your ability to handle life's challenges effectively.

When you blend persistence, upskilling, and enhanced emotional intelligence, you've got a potent combination. It's like you've been walking in circles and now you're set to launch. You've got the drive to keep going (persistence), the skills to move faster and more efficiently (upskilling), and the wisdom to know where you're going and how to get there (emotional intelligence). Together, they give you the push you need to enter a new orbit – a better path leading towards your goals, dreams, and a more fulfilling life.

The Analogy of Water Reaching Boiling Point

The process of continuous self-improvement can be likened to the journey water takes to reach its boiling point. When you commit to learning new things (upskilling) and stick with your goals (persistence), it's like adding fuel to your reservoir, gallon by gallon.

Think of it this way: as you keep learning and growing, every new skill you acquire and every bit of effort you put into understanding yourself and those around you adds a little more to your performance.

It's a slow process, and just like water heating on the stove, there isn't a sudden change at first. But you're filling up; you're moving closer to that critical point.

When you hit the 100th degree, the point where water turns into steam, that's when the transformation happens. This change represents the significant shifts in your life due to your hard work and dedication to self-improvement. Just as steam has the power to propel engines, turbines, and ships forward, the skills you've developed enable you to overcome obstacles, advance your career, and manage personal relationships more effectively.

This analogy underscores the incredible power of continuous self-improvement. Just as it takes a consistent source of heat to bring water to its boiling point and transform it into steam, it requires ongoing effort and dedication to reach new heights in your personal and professional life. But once you reach your full capacity, the 100th degree for you, that little spark can ignite and launch you like a rocket, allowing you to rise to new heights and reach your targeted goals.

The Impact of Changing Orbits

When you shift to a higher orbit in life, you start to encounter new "satellites" - in this context, we're talking about friends, colleagues, and other connections. There's a popular idea that you are, in essence, an average of the five people you spend the most time with. This suggests that the people closest to you have a significant influence on various aspects of your life, from your income and fitness levels to your social engagements and overall outlook on life.

To understand who these five pivotal individuals are in your own life, a good starting point could be to examine your phone's call log, text messages, emails, social media interactions, and even photos from gatherings. You might find that these individuals mirror your current lifestyle, aspirations, and perhaps even challenges.

As you elevate to a new orbit, the nature of your relationships and the people you interact with regularly might begin to shift. This isn't just about seeking out people who are where you aspire to be, but also about naturally aligning with individuals who share your new interests, goals, and habits as you pursue personal growth and development.

This evolution in your social circle is critical because the influences around you can significantly impact your motivation, perspectives, and choices. Being surrounded by individuals who reflect the qualities you aspire to can inspire you to maintain your trajectory, push your limits, and continue growing. In contrast, remaining in a circle that doesn't evolve with you might limit your growth potential.

In essence, as you change your orbit and start moving in a new direction, your world expands. You begin to form connections with individuals who not only reflect your current state but also embody the future you're working toward. This network of new satellites doesn't just represent a change in your social circle; it symbolises the broader transformation in your life, encouraging you to keep pushing forward and exploring new heights.

Strategies for Orbit Shift

Shifting your orbit means consciously changing your daily routines and the company you keep to foster personal growth and reach new heights. This transformation is similar to nurturing a seed in optimal conditions for it to sprout and flourish. Just as the right mix of soil, water, sunlight, and temperature is crucial for a seed's growth, the environment we cultivate around ourselves—comprising our habits, routines, and social interactions—plays a significant role in our personal development.

Evaluating Your Current Orbit: Begin by examining your daily life. Look at what you do every day and who you spend your time with. This will help you see which parts of your life are pushing you forward and which are holding you back.

Setting Clear Goals: Knowing what you want out of life, both personally and professionally, is crucial. These goals act as a compass, guiding the changes you need to make in your daily habits and social circle.

Introducing New Habits: Align your daily actions with your goals. Whether it's adopting a healthier lifestyle or learning skills for professional advancement, each new habit brings you a step closer to the orbit you desire.

Seeking Out Positive Influences: Surround yourself with people who reflect where you want to be. Expanding your circle to include those who inspire and encourage you is vital. They are like the sunlight and water that help a plant grow.

Engaging in New Activities: Dive into groups or activities that resonate with your interests and aspirations. This can lead you to like-minded individuals who can positively impact your journey.

Limiting Negative Influences: Just as plants can be choked by weeds, negative people can hinder your growth. Making a conscious decision to spend less time with such individuals is crucial for your development.

Reflecting and Adjusting: Growth is an ongoing process. Regularly take stock of your progress and be open to making necessary adjustments. This flexibility is key to navigating your way to a higher orbit.

Incorporating these strategies isn't about hoping for a better life; it's about actively building it. It involves creating the right conditions for your growth, much like ensuring a plant has what it needs to thrive. By consciously choosing who you surround yourself with and how you spend your time, you directly influence your life's trajectory. Friends and acquaintances are like the climate around a plant—they can either nurture its growth or stunt it. Thus, selecting your social circle with care is as crucial as choosing the right soil for a seed.

This approach empowers you to move beyond mere hopes for a better future into actively shaping it, ensuring that your environment—the sum of your habits, routines, and social interactions—fosters the growth and achievement you aspire to.

A New Trajectory

When you decide to change how you live and think, aiming for better things in life, you're starting a new kind of journey. This path is about growing personally and professionally. It's about doing things differently, learning new ways to handle challenges, and being around people who bring out the best in you.

Changing your life's path means you're also changing who influences you. When you surround yourself with positive influences, you'll notice that the quality of your life improves. It's like having friends, family, or mentors who not only support you but also push you to be your best. Over time, you'll see that you're doing better than before because the people around you are helping you grow.

This journey to a new path isn't just for now; it's for the future too. The benefits of making these changes in your life will last a long time. You'll build stronger connections with people, become more flexible and able to handle whatever life throws at you, and find more satisfaction in pursuing goals that really matter to you.

So, think of this as your moment to start something new. It might seem a bit scary or challenging at first, but the rewards—like feeling more fulfilled, advancing in your career, and leading a richer life—are definitely worth it. Aim for this new direction and let it lead you to places you've always wanted to go.

"Change is inevitable, but transformation is a choice" Heather Ash Amara

Chapter 7

Fear and Failure

Fear and failure are parts of life that everyone experiences. It's important to understand that these aren't just obstacles to avoid but are actually key to personal growth when managed well.

Let's talk about fear first. Fear is a feeling that comes up when we're stepping into the unknown or facing a challenge. It's totally natural and happens to everyone. Think of it as a signal your mind gives you, saying, "Hey, pay attention, this is important." But the thing about fear is, if we let it take over, it can stop us from doing things we really want or need to do.

Now, onto failure. Failure happens when we try something and it doesn't work out the way we hoped. Just like fear, failure isn't something to shy away from. In fact, every time we fail, we learn something. It's through trying and not always succeeding that we figure out how to do things better next time.

Managing fear and failure doesn't mean never feeling scared or never messing up. It means learning how to move forward despite those feelings. It's about taking what we learn from our fears and failures and using it to do better in the future.

Understanding Fear: Think of fear like a shadow. It's always around, especially when you're facing something new or challenging. But like a shadow, fear doesn't have the power to stop you unless you let it. Fear comes from thinking too much about what might go wrong. While it's normal to feel fear, it's something you can learn to manage. You can't get rid of it completely, but you can keep it from taking over.

Think about fear as a reaction. It's your brain's way of trying to protect you, telling you to be careful because it sees something as a threat. But sometimes, our brain can get a little too protective and see threats where there aren't any. That's when fear starts to feel like a big shadow hanging over us, even though the actual risk might not be that big.

Understanding fear means recognizing it for what it is: a natural feeling that everyone experiences. It's not a sign that we're weak or that we can't handle challenges. Instead, it's just our mind trying to keep us safe. But, just like a shadow, fear doesn't have any power on its own. It only feels powerful because of how we react to it.

By realizing that fear is often the result of our thoughts, we can start to control how much it affects us. Instead of letting it stop us from doing things, we can acknowledge it, understand why it's there, and then make a decision to move forward anyway.

Managing Fear:

Managing fear is about finding ways to deal with it, focusing on preparation and changing the way we think about fear. We can't always get rid of fear completely, but we can control how much it influences us.

One key strategy is to prepare. For example, if you're nervous about giving a presentation, practicing and knowing your material well can reduce fear. Preparation builds confidence because it makes you feel more ready to face the situation.

Another important approach is to adjust how you think about fear. Instead of seeing it as something that stops you, think of it as a normal reaction that you can handle. Remind yourself that feeling scared doesn't mean you can't do something; it just means you're about to do something challenging or new.

It's also helpful to gradually expose yourself to what scares you. Start with smaller challenges and work your way up. This can help reduce fear over time because you're proving to yourself that you can handle these situations.

Take Small Steps: If something feels overwhelming, break it down. Start with smaller, less intimidating tasks related to your fear and gradually increase the challenge as you feel more comfortable.

Practice Mindfulness: Focus on the present moment rather than worrying about what might happen. Techniques like deep breathing, meditation, or yoga can help calm your mind.

Talk About It: Sharing your fears with someone can lighten the load. A friend, family member, or therapist can offer support and perspective.

Learn from Past Experiences: Reflect on times when you faced your fears and succeeded. What worked? How did you feel afterward? Use these insights to boost your confidence.

Visualize Success: Instead of imagining the worst-case scenario, try to picture a positive outcome. Visualizing success can help create a more optimistic mindset.

Be Kind to Yourself: Self-compassion is key. Don't beat yourself up for feeling scared. Acknowledge your feelings, and then gently encourage yourself to take the next step.

Fear in Childhood vs. Adulthood: When we were kids, managing fear seemed easier. We didn't connect our self-worth to our successes or failures. Falling while learning to walk wasn't a source of shame; it was just part of the process. We didn't wait to be perfect at something before giving it a try. Whether it was speaking, writing, drawing, or painting, we jumped in, not worried about our reputation.

This fearless approach allowed us to learn and grow freely. The focus was on the experience, not the outcome. This is how we naturally managed fear: by doing, learning, and gradually getting better without the burden of judgment.

However, as we grow into adults, this changes. We become more conscious of our identities and how others perceive us. There's a pressure to present ourselves as perfect, to get things right on the first try. This fear of judgment or failure can stop us from taking risks or trying new things, especially when we feel like we're under the watchful eye of the world.

The way to manage fear in adulthood shifts towards preparation. Gaining knowledge and preparing ourselves for new challenges can give us the confidence we need to face our fears. For example, we wouldn't drive without first taking lessons and getting a license because the risks involved are much higher. This preparation helps us manage fear by giving us the tools and skills we need to succeed, reducing the unknowns that can fuel fear.

Being prepared and educated on a task makes us less fearful. It's not about being fearless in the sense of ignoring dangers but about being fear-less by reducing the unknown through learning and practice. A well-prepared individual approaches challenges with confidence, not because they're certain of success but because they're equipped to handle the process and learn from it, regardless of the outcome.

Failure as Feedback: Failure is like getting feedback, not the end of the road. It tells you what didn't work so you can figure out how to do better next time. Some people say that failure is all in your head and you shouldn't worry about it. But that's easier said than done, right? Most of us aren't like Buddha, with perfect wisdom to just brush off failure without a second thought.

When we fail at something, it provides clear evidence of where our efforts fell short and where there's room for improvement. It's like getting specific pointers on what to work on next. This perspective encourages a mindset of continuous learning and adaptability. Instead of getting stuck thinking we're just not good at something, we ask ourselves, "What can I learn from this? How can I do better next time?"

This approach to failure helps build resilience. Instead of fearing failure and avoiding challenges, we become more willing to try new things, knowing that even if we don't succeed, we'll gain insights that can help us in the future. We start to see each attempt, successful or not, as a step forward in our journey of personal and professional development.

Redefining failure as feedback emphasizes the process of growth over the need for perfection. It's about valuing progress and learning over always needing to be right or successful on the first try. This can lead to a more fulfilling and less stressful experience in all areas of life, as we become more open to trying, failing, and ultimately succeeding.

Childhood Lessons

Reflecting on childhood, we can see how our approach to learning and failure was fundamentally different. As kids, we saw failure not as a setback but as a natural step toward getting better at something. Remember trying to ride a bike? Each fall wasn't a sign to give up; it was a part of the process, a moment to learn what went wrong and how to keep balance better next time.

This perspective on failure as a child was liberating. It allowed us to embrace new challenges with an open heart, knowing that stumbling was just part of learning. There was no shame in falling down or not getting it right immediately because the goal was always about getting better, not being perfect from the start.

This childhood lesson is a powerful reminder that mastery comes through practice, patience, and persistence. Each attempt, each failure, was a step closer to understanding and improvement. We didn't fear new tasks or give up after the first try. Instead, we were motivated by curiosity and the joy of eventual success.

Understanding Failure in Adulthood

Growing up changes how we see ourselves. We often try to look perfect, acting as if we can do everything right the first time. This is like wearing a mask to hide any flaws we think we have. The problem is, when we're scared of failing, especially where others can see, it feels like we're risking showing a side of ourselves we're not proud of.

Thinking about failing makes us more scared of it. It's like blowing up a balloon; the more we worry, the bigger and scarier it gets. This fear can stop us from trying new things because we don't want to fail and have others see us in a bad light.

But there's a way to deal with this. Realizing we're the ones making our fear bigger is the first step. Remembering that it's normal to fail sometimes helps too. Failures aren't the whole story of who we are. They're just moments that happen to everyone.

Starting with small steps can help. Trying little things and seeing it's okay to fail sometimes can make us feel better. We learn a bit from each try, whether we succeed or not. Slowly, this helps us worry less about failing.

If we can stop trying to look perfect all the time and accept that it's okay to mess up, we'll start to feel better about trying new things. Sharing our stories of when things didn't go as planned can help others feel okay about their failures too. This makes everyone feel more comfortable with trying, failing, and trying again.

By seeing our mistakes as chances to learn, we can drop our fear of failing and start enjoying trying new things more. And when we do this, we grow and find more happiness in our lives.

Strategies for Overcoming Fear and Accepting Failure

Navigating through fear and failure is like learning to ride a bike. At first, it seems daunting, but with practice, you find your balance. Let's explore strategies that can help us overcome fear and accept failure as part of our growth journey.

Preparation as a Tool

Think about preparation as packing a backpack for a hike. The better you pack, the more confident and capable you feel tackling the trail ahead. Similarly, thorough preparation for any challenge works wonders. It builds your confidence and sharpens your skills, making the once intimidating task seem more manageable.

For instance, if you're worried about public speaking, practicing your speech several times can make a big difference. Each rehearsal gives you a firmer grasp of your material and a boost in confidence. Preparation doesn't make the challenge disappear, but it equips you to face it head-on.

From Fear to Fearlessness

Overcoming fear isn't about never feeling scared; it's about learning to move forward even when you are. Everyone has a story of a time they felt stuck because of fear. But many also have stories of facing that fear and coming out stronger.

Consider someone who's afraid of heights but dreams of mountain climbing. They might start small, perhaps by climbing a ladder, then a hill, and gradually working up to higher peaks. Each step is a victory, a testament to their growing courage and determination.

Such stories teach us valuable lessons. They show that moving from fear to fearlessness is a journey, one small step at a time. And as we take these steps, we transform our fear into determination.

Emotional Resilience and Recovery

Building emotional resilience is like strengthening a muscle; it requires time and effort. It's about developing a toughness that helps you bounce back from setbacks. When you're resilient, a failure doesn't end your journey; it becomes a detour, perhaps leading to an even better path.

To build resilience, start by adjusting your outlook. View each setback as a learning opportunity. Instead of dwelling on what went wrong, ask yourself, "What can I learn from this?" This mindset helps reduce the sting of failure and prepares you for future challenges.

Emotional recovery is also key. Allow yourself to feel upset about a failure, but don't let it consume you. Practice self-care, whether that's talking to a friend, going for a walk, or engaging in a hobby. These activities can help you regain your balance and perspective.

Finally, persistence is crucial. Remember the old saying, "If at first, you don't succeed, try, try again." There's a lot of truth in those words. Success often comes not from avoiding failure but from facing it, learning from it, and pressing on.

For Example,

Mary Kom's story shows how she faced fear and recovered from what seemed like failures. She's a great example of being strong and determined. Her life isn't just about winning in boxing but also about how she dealt with challenges in her personal and professional life. Mary grew up in a small village in Manipur, India. At first, she kept her boxing a secret from her family because it wasn't common for women to do it. This shows how she faced and overcame the fear of being judged by society and her family.

After reaching big goals, she faced a tough test when she became a mom. Balancing being a mom with her busy job was hard. Some people thought she'd have to give up her career when she became a mom. But she didn't give up. She got ready even more and came back to boxing with more determination. In 2010, she won at the World Amateur Boxing Championships after becoming a mom. This win showed she could beat fear and failure. It wasn't just a win for her, but it showed that tough times can lead to big achievements.

In 2011, during the Asian Cup Women's Boxing Tournament in China, Mary Kom faced a heart-wrenching dilemma. Her son was undergoing critical cardiac surgery back home due to congenital heart disease, a condition where the heart has defects that impair its normal function. This surgery was crucial as congenital heart disease can significantly impact a child's survival and quality of life.

Mary Kom, at the pinnacle of her career, was set to face the then-Asian Champion, Kim Myong Sim, in the finals. The entire nation's hopes were pinned on her, yet her heart was with her son in the hospital. After discussing with her husband, K Onler Kom, she made the difficult decision to compete in the finals, encouraged by her husband's belief in her hard work and the importance of the match.

Mary fought bravely and won the gold medal, demonstrating incredible fortitude and dedication. Simultaneously, her son's surgery was successful. Upon returning to India, the first thing Mary did was rush to the hospital to be by her son's side in the ICU.

In a heartfelt conversation with the Press Trust of India, K Onler Kom expressed his pride in Mary's achievement and acknowledged the difficulty of the decision she made to leave their son at such a critical time. He shared that when their son was informed about his mother's victory, he was happy and proud of her.

Mary Kom shows us how to conquer fear: admit it, get ready to tackle it, and keep moving towards your goals despite challenges. She motivates us to see obstacles as chances to learn and mistakes as ways to get better, not as reasons to quit. Her story is a strong reminder for anyone facing fear or failure - with bravery, persistence, and preparation, you can beat any obstacle. Think of failure as a friend, one who might be a bit tough to get along with at first but ultimately guides us toward success. Just like a snake charmer who skillfully handles poisonous snakes, a mahout who confidently rides an elephant, or a ringmaster who tames lions, it's not the size of the challenge that defines us but the skills we acquire to overcome it.

Upskilling is the key to managing fear. When we learn and grow, we equip ourselves with the tools needed to face any challenge head-on. *This doesn't make the challenge any smaller or less threatening; instead, it makes us bigger, better, and more capable of handling whatever comes our way.*

Chapter 8

Never Settle

Curiosity is like a spark that's there in all of us when we're kids. It's this amazing feeling that makes us want to know more about everything around us. Imagine being a little kid again, looking at the world with wide eyes, wanting to touch, see, and understand everything. That's curiosity at work. Kids don't worry about whether they're strong enough or smart enough; they just want to learn. They're not afraid of what others might think if they ask a question or get something wrong. This fearless way of exploring is something special about being young.

Think about it: kids dive into life ready to discover new things. They don't need someone to tell them it's okay to be curious; they just are. This natural drive to explore and understand doesn't care about mistakes or judgments. It's all about the adventure of finding out what's out there.

This curiosity isn't just playing around; it's how kids learn so fast. They might not know it, but every time they ask 'why?' or 'how?' they're building their understanding of the world. It's this endless questioning and experimenting that helps them pick up new skills without even trying hard. They're like little scientists, testing out their theories about how things work, learning from what happens, and then trying again.

As adults, we sometimes forget how to be this curious. We might worry too much about getting things right or what others will think. But deep down, we all have this natural instinct to learn and explore, just like when we were kids. Remembering this can help us keep learning and growing, no matter how old we get. It's about bringing back that sense of wonder and being open to new experiences, just like a child discovering the world for the first time.

This natural way kids approach learning—with excitement and without fear—is a big nudge for us grown-ups. It makes us think: Have we let our worries or what others might think stop us from trying new things? Keeping that spark of curiosity alive is super important. This "never settle" attitude that children naturally possess is a reminder of the importance of maintaining a lifelong curiosity.

For Example, a kid stepping onto a cricket field for the first time. They're holding a bat, not quite sure of the rules or the correct way to grip it, yet eager to play. With eyes fixed on the ball, they take a swing. Sometimes they miss, and other times they manage a slight connection, sending the ball rolling a few feet away.

Each attempt, whether a miss or a minor hit, is an adventure. They're learning—the stance feels more natural, the concept of timing becomes clearer, and even the misses teach them something about how to anticipate the ball's path. There's no concern for perfection here, no shadow of professional standards looming over them. The joy comes from the game itself, from the feel of the bat in their hands, and from the anticipation of making contact with the ball.

This child, through their play, is standing for the essence of curiosity. Every swing at the ball, successful or not, lifts their understanding and skill. This is not just about playing cricket; it's a lesson in growth and learning. Mistakes aren't setbacks; they're stepping stones. With each round, the child's skills get sharper, their understanding deeper, and their love for the game grows. They're driven by a pure desire to explore and improve, one swing at a time.

Just like the kid on the cricket field, we all started life with a spark of curiosity. However, as we got older, the world around us started to shape how we think and feel. We learned about what's logical and what's not, started to understand our own egos, and became aware of our limitations. Slowly, without even realizing it, many of us began to put our curiosity aside. We started to feel more comfortable sticking with what we know, settling into our routines, and becoming complacent.

This shift isn't something that happens overnight. It's the result of countless small moments—maybe being told our questions were silly, or learning to fear making mistakes because of how others might react. Over time, these experiences can build up, making us more cautious and less willing to step out of our comfort zones. We might start to worry more about getting things right or fitting in, rather than exploring new possibilities and learning from the process.

This tendency to pull back from curiosity is reinforced by societal expectations. We're often encouraged to find a "practical" path, to focus on success in conventional terms. The wide-eyed wonder we started with can seem out of place in a world that values certainty and expertise. But in doing so, we lose out on the joy and growth that come from asking questions and trying new things, even if it means facing the unknown.

Reconnecting with that innate curiosity means challenging these pressures and self-imposed limitations. It involves giving ourselves permission to wonder, to experiment, and to be okay with not having all the answers. By acknowledging that it's fine to be a beginner again, to learn and grow in new directions, we can start to break down the barriers that have kept us from fully exploring our potential.

Challenging the Status Quo

Challenging the status quo means taking a hard look at where you are now and asking yourself if this is really where you want to be. It's about questioning the usual way you do things and the usual thoughts you think. This isn't easy. It means stepping outside your comfort zone and facing the unknown. And while you might turn to Google for answers to many questions, this journey of self-discovery and reigniting your passion for learning is something that search engines can't do for you.

To reignite your zeal for learning and experimentation, start by identifying areas in your life or knowledge you've always been curious about but never explored. Maybe it's a hobby you've put off, a skill you've wanted to develop, or a subject you've wanted to study. This curiosity is your guide, pointing you toward the paths less traveled in your life.

Next, give yourself permission to be a beginner again. Accept the process of learning, knowing that it's okay not to have all the answers right away. Remember, every expert was once a beginner. This mindset frees you from the fear of making mistakes and allows you to see each attempt, successful or not, as a valuable step in your learning journey.

Moreover, create opportunities for experimentation in your daily life. This could mean setting aside time each week to try something new, joining a class or group that focuses on a topic of interest, or simply changing up your routine to break out of autopilot mode. Experimentation leads to discovery, and discovery fuels further curiosity and learning.

By challenging how things are usually done, you're not just looking for change for the sake of change. You're on the lookout for deeper meaning in your life and a better understanding of what makes you tick. This search for new experiences and knowledge is what keeps things interesting and helps you grow as a person. Remember, the biggest thing stopping you from trying new things is often your own worries about what might happen if you do. Pushing past these fears can open up a whole new world of possibilities.

Beyond Comfort Zones

Stepping beyond comfort zones is crucial if we're aiming for growth. Often, we build walls around ourselves made of what we think is logical, our ego, and what we believe are our limits. These walls can keep us from trying new things or taking risks because we're trying to protect ourselves from failure or embarrassment.

To move past these barriers, the first step is acknowledging they exist. Recognize that sometimes what we consider 'logical' might just be an excuse to stay safe. Our ego can trick us into thinking we need to maintain a certain image, stopping us from taking steps that might show vulnerability. And those limits we think we have? They're often not as solid as we believe.

Breaking down these barriers starts with a simple question: "What would I try if I knew I couldn't fail?" Letting go of the fear of failure and the need for constant success opens up a world of possibilities. It's about giving yourself permission to fail and to learn from those failures.

A practical approach to stepping out of your comfort zone is to start small. Choose one thing you've been avoiding because of these barriers and take a step towards it. Maybe it's signing up for a class in something you're interested in but worried you're not good at, or perhaps it's reaching out to someone you admire but have been too intimidated to talk to.

The key is to recognize that growth comes from stepping into the unknown and embracing the lessons that come with it, not from staying in the safety of what we already know. By pushing past the barriers of logic, ego, and perceived limitations, we open ourselves up to new experiences, skills, and a deeper understanding of who we are and what we're capable of.

The Journey from Ignorance to Awareness

The journey from not knowing what we don't know to recognizing our gaps in knowledge is a crucial step towards personal growth. This process starts when we first acknowledge that our understanding of the world, and even ourselves, is limited. It's like realizing there are whole areas of a map you've never explored or even knew existed.

Self-awareness acts as the guide on this journey. It's the tool that helps us see where we are on the map and highlights the uncharted territories we have yet to explore. With self-awareness, we start to see our strengths and weaknesses more clearly. It's like turning on a light in a room that's been dark, revealing both the treasures and the clutter within.

This newfound awareness is what propels us forward. It encourages us to venture into new areas of knowledge and skill, pushing us beyond the familiar. As we explore these new territories, we often discover hidden talents and passions that were previously obscured by our own ignorance. It's akin to finding hidden gems in a landscape we thought we knew well.

Moving from not knowing to being more aware is a big change. It's not just about learning new things; it's about understanding ourselves better. This process helps us see what we're really good at and where we could use some improvement. It's kind of like finding hidden treasures in ourselves that we didn't know were there. These discoveries can lead us to new opportunities for both personal and work-related growth that we might not have considered before.

Being self-aware means more than just knowing where you stand right now. It's about always being on the lookout for new things to learn and new ways to grow. It's the starting point for building a life that's full of learning and getting better, bit by bit. This journey of discovery is how we keep evolving and becoming the best versions of ourselves. It's about not staying still, always moving forward, and being open to finding out more about who we are and what we can do.

Self-awareness serves as a foundation

Self-awareness is like laying down the first stone when you're building a skyscraper. It's the foundation that everything else rests upon when we're talking about personal growth and exploration. With self-awareness, you start to recognize where you're starting from – it's realizing what you know and, more importantly, what you don't know yet. This realization is key because it shifts you from a place of not knowing what you're missing out on to a state where you're aware there's more to learn and discover.

By acknowledging the gaps in our knowledge and skills, we open the door to exploring new areas. This could mean diving into subjects or activities we've never considered before or finally pursuing interests we've put on the back burner. As we explore these new grounds, we often stumble upon talents and passions we didn't know we had. It's like finding hidden gems within ourselves that only come to light because we were brave enough to venture into the unknown.

This journey from "you don't know what you don't know" to "you know what you don't know" is crucial. It marks the beginning of a path filled with learning and self-discovery. The more we understand about ourselves, the better equipped we are to make choices that align with our true potential and desires. Self-awareness doesn't just help us see where we are now; it points us towards where we want to go and unlocks the potential within us that we might never have realized existed. It's the key to living a life that's not only about reaching goals but also about continuous growth and fulfillment.

Embracing Small Beginnings

Starting small in the journey of self-improvement is like the process of evolving from a simple single-rotor drone to a sophisticated GPS-enabled drone. At first, you might only be able to hover a few feet off the ground, struggling with the basics and feeling limited in what you can achieve. This stage, though, is crucial. It's your foundation, your launching pad. It's tempting to want to skip straight to becoming a rocket, but real growth requires patience and taking one small step at a time.

Beginning as a single-rotor drone, you learn the fundamentals: how to stay balanced, navigate simple obstacles, and respond to controls. These initial skills are essential. As you get better, you evolve into a multi-rotor drone, gaining stability and the ability to maneuver with more precision. Each step forward builds on the last, preparing you for the next level of complexity and capability.

When you finally become a GPS drone, you're not just flying; you're navigating with precision, adjusting your path based on real-time data, and reaching destinations you couldn't have imagined when you started. But to get there, you need to pay attention to the "weather" of your life—the conditions that affect your journey. This means checking in with yourself, assessing your environment, understanding the challenges you face, and adapting your approach accordingly.

This analogy reminds us that every expert was once a beginner, and every sophisticated skill set started with basic building blocks. The key is not to rush the process but to embrace each stage of development, learn from it, and use it as a stepping stone to the next level. By starting small and staying committed to continuous learning and adaptation, you unlock your full potential and achieve goals that once seemed out of reach.

Just as a drone pilot must adjust for weather, wind, and other external conditions to ensure a successful flight, we too must be attuned to the environments that surround us in our personal and professional lives. The metaphor of navigating a drone through changing weather conditions is a powerful illustration of how we should approach our own journeys of growth and development.

In life, "weather" can represent the ever-changing circumstances we encounter—be it in our jobs, our relationships, or our personal goals. "Wind direction" and "velocity" might symbolize the challenges and obstacles that come our way, while "visibility," "sunshine," and "rain" could reflect the clarity (or lack thereof) with which we see our path forward, the good times that motivate us, and the difficult periods that test our resilience.

The importance of assessing these conditions lies in our ability to adapt. Just as a drone might need to change its course in response to a sudden gust of wind, we might need to adjust our plans when faced with unexpected challenges. This might mean reevaluating our goals, learning new skills, seeking advice, or even changing direction entirely.

Adapting to external conditions doesn't mean giving up at the first sign of difficulty. Instead, it's about being flexible and resourceful, understanding that the path to our goals isn't always straight. It's about making informed decisions that take into account the current "weather" of our lives. By doing so, we not only navigate through challenges more effectively but also open ourselves up to opportunities and experiences we might have missed had we rigidly stuck to our initial course.

Cultivating a Never-Settle Attitude

Cultivating a never-settle attitude is about developing a mindset that always pushes you to grow, learn, and exceed your own expectations. It's about refusing to become complacent or to accept mediocrity in any area of your life. Here are some strategies to help maintain that continuous drive:

Set Clear, Challenging Goals: Define what success looks like for you in different areas of your life, and make sure your goals are both ambitious and achievable. Break them down into smaller, manageable tasks to keep you motivated and on track.

Accept Learning as a Lifelong Process: Understand that there's always something new to learn, no matter how much you already know. Seek out resources, courses, and mentors that can help you gain new skills and knowledge.

Seek Feedback and Constructive Criticism: Be open to feedback from others, as it can provide valuable insights into areas you may need to improve. Use it as a tool for growth rather than taking it personally.

Celebrate Small Wins: Recognize and celebrate your progress, even if it's just a small step towards a bigger goal. This helps build momentum and keeps you motivated.

Surround Yourself with High Achievers: Spend time with people who inspire you and push you to be your best. Their drive and success can motivate you to raise your own standards.

Reflect and Adjust: Regularly take time to reflect on your progress. Be honest with yourself about what's working and what isn't, and be willing to adjust your approach as needed.

Stay Resilient in the Face of Setbacks: Understand that setbacks are a natural part of the growth process. Instead of letting them discourage you, use them as learning opportunities and bounce back even stronger.

Keep Your End Goal in Mind: Always remind yourself of the bigger picture and why you're working so hard. This can help you stay focused and driven, even when things get tough.

Adopting a new mindset is crucial when it comes to learning new skills and reaching your full potential. It's about telling yourself, "I can do more, and I can be more," and really believing it. This shift in how you think about yourself and your abilities opens up a world where you're not limited by past achievements or failures. Instead, you're driven by what you could accomplish next.

Changing your mindset means seeing every challenge as an opportunity to grow rather than a barrier that holds you back. It's about choosing to learn a variety of skills, not just sticking to what you already know. This could mean trying things you've never done before, like learning a new language, picking up a musical instrument, or coding, even if it feels out of your comfort zone at first.

Here's the key: don't settle for "I'm just okay" at something when you have the potential to be great. This new way of thinking encourages you not only to start new journeys of learning but also to stick with them, pushing through the tough parts until you see progress. It's about not giving up on yourself and always striving for the best version of you.

So, remember, adopting a changed mindset isn't just about adding new skills to your repertoire; it's about changing how you view yourself and your capabilities. It's a powerful tool that motivates you to chase after what you're truly capable of, ensuring you never settle for less than you deserve.

Becoming a Multi-Disciplinary Master

The process of acquiring new skills and growing personally can be likened to training to become a Multi Martial Arts (MMA) fighter. Just as an MMA fighter needs to learn and master a variety of combat skills to be prepared for any situation in the ring, embracing a diverse set of skills in life prepares you for various challenges and opportunities.

When you decide to expand your abilities and not settle for the status quo, you're committing to a journey of continuous improvement and adaptation. An MMA fighter doesn't focus on just one discipline; they integrate techniques from boxing, wrestling, judo, and more. This diversity makes them more versatile and prepared for whatever their opponent might throw at them.

Similarly, when you broaden your skillset beyond what you're currently comfortable with, you become more versatile and capable of handling different situations in life. Learning new languages, mastering new technologies, or even developing softer skills like public speaking or leadership can make you more adaptable and resilient.

Moreover, MMA fighters are known for their fitness and swiftness, qualities that are developed through rigorous training and discipline. This physical and mental preparedness is akin to the personal growth that comes from pushing your boundaries and learning new skills. It's not just about the skills themselves but about developing the perseverance, discipline, and mental agility to learn and apply them effectively.

Envisioning yourself as an MMA fighter in the arena of life can be a powerful motivator. It's a reminder that being armed with a wide range of skills, and continually seeking to add more, not only makes you more capable but also ensures you never settle for less than you can achieve. Just like MMA fighters, you become equipped to face challenges head-on, adapt to change, and seize opportunities with confidence and skill.

Being versatile, fit, and swift offers significant advantages, much like the diverse skills of an MMA fighter prepare them for various challenges in the ring. In both personal and professional aspects of life, these qualities translate into being well-equipped to handle unexpected situations, adapt to change, and make quick, informed decisions.

Versatility means having a broad skill set, allowing you to tackle different tasks and roles effectively. In your personal life, this could mean being able to fix a leaky faucet, plan a weekend getaway, or support a friend through a tough time. Professionally, versatility might manifest as the ability to manage projects, understand new software quickly, or communicate effectively with different teams. This adaptability makes you valuable and resilient, able to thrive in diverse environments.

Fitness, both mental and physical, is crucial for maintaining high energy levels and resilience. Physically, staying active keeps your body healthy and ready to take on the day's challenges. Mentally, fitness could mean practicing mindfulness or problem-solving exercises, which keep your mind sharp and prepared for whatever comes your way. This preparedness is vital, whether you're facing a personal challenge or a professional deadline.

Swiftness involves reacting promptly and effectively to situations. It's about making quick decisions without sacrificing accuracy—a skill that's incredibly valuable whether you're navigating personal dilemmas or making strategic choices in a fast-paced work environment. Being swift doesn't mean rushing through decisions; it's about efficiently processing information and taking decisive action.

Having lots of skills, being in good shape both in your body and mind, and being able to think and act quickly are super useful, no matter what you're doing. They help you deal with all sorts of situations better and keep you moving forward.

Remember that the path to never settling is one of constant motion—of seeking, learning, and transcending the familiar. It's a commitment to push beyond the boundaries of what we know, to explore what could be, and to embody the resilience and adaptability of a seasoned fighter. In our personal and professional lives, these principles guide us to not just achieve our goals but to redefine them, always aiming higher, always exploring further.

Conclusion

It's time for you to start your own journey of change. Remember, this journey is as much about the experiences you have along the way as it is about where you end up. It's about growing, learning, and becoming the best version of yourself.

Think of this journey as a road trip. You might have a final destination in mind, but the adventures you have, the people you meet, and the challenges you overcome while getting there are what truly matter. These experiences shape you, teach you, and sometimes even redefine your destination.

Starting this journey requires bravery. It's about being open to change, ready to learn, and willing to face challenges head-on. Your journey will be unique, filled with its own set of ups and downs. But remember, every step forward, even the ones that seem like setbacks, is part of your growth.

So, take that first step today. Accept the changes that come your way with a spirit of curiosity and a heart full of courage. Keep improving, not just in what you do but in who you are. Your persistence, your ability to understand yourself and others, and your drive to keep moving forward will be your companions on this journey.

The path ahead is yours to choose. Start your transformation journey now, knowing that the real treasure is in the journey itself and the person you become along the way.

Imagine you decide to take your personal and professional growth seriously. What could happen? Picture yourself a few years from now, having consistently worked on improving yourself, learning new skills, and facing challenges head-on.

First, you'll likely find yourself achieving things you might not have thought possible. This could mean getting that job profile you always wanted, expanding your business to greater heights, or finally feeling confident in your abilities. It's not just about career success, though. On a personal level, you might find yourself more fulfilled, with deeper relationships and a better understanding of who you are and what you truly value.

You could also become a source of inspiration for others. People around you—friends, family, colleagues—might see the changes in you and feel motivated to embark on their own journeys of self-improvement. Your growth could create a ripple effect, positively impacting your community.

Moreover, the skills and emotional intelligence you develop will help you navigate life's ups and downs more effectively. Whether it's dealing with stress, managing conflicts, or making tough decisions, you'll be better equipped to handle whatever comes your way.

Committing to this journey of growth is about more than just the accolades or achievements; it's about becoming a more resilient, insightful, and compassionate person. The potential outcomes are vast and varied, but they all start with a choice to invest in yourself today.

A Final Word

As we reach the end of this journey through the chapters, let's pause to reflect on the core principles that have guided us: the willingness to accept change, the commitment to continuous improvement, and the power of persistence. These are not just ideas to ponder; they are the bedrock upon which you can build a life of fulfilment, growth, and achievement.

Accepting change is the first step towards any form of growth. The world around us is always evolving, and so are we. Embracing change rather than resisting it allows us to flow with life's currents, leading to unexpected and often rewarding destinations.

Continuous improvement is a lifelong endeavor. There is no final level of mastery or a point at which learning stops. The pursuit of knowledge, skills, and emotional growth is what keeps life vibrant and engaging. It's about always striving to be a better version of yourself than you were yesterday.

Finally, the power of persistence cannot be overstated. The path to achieving your goals is rarely straight or smooth. It will have its share of obstacles and challenges. However, it's your persistence in the face of these trials that will define your journey. Persistence is the force that turns failure into feedback, challenges into opportunities, and dreams into reality.

As you close this book and look towards your future, remember that your journey is uniquely yours. There will be highs and lows, successes and setbacks, but each experience offers valuable lessons. Stay open to change, committed to improving, and persistent in your endeavours. The journey ahead is rich with potential, waiting for you to shape it.

Here's to the journey ahead—may it be one of continuous growth, discovery, and personal fulfilment.

Notes

www.ingramcontent.com/pod-product-compliance
Lightning Source LLC
LaVergne TN
LVHW091111150826
845673LV00002B/778

* 9 7 9 8 8 9 4 4 6 0 6 9 7 *